ALL GOOD

and

ABSOLUTE BEGINNERS

All Good Men
and
Absolute Beginners

Two Plays for Television
by

TREVOR GRIFFITHS

FABER AND FABER

3 Queen Square

London

First published in 1977
by Faber and Faber Limited
3 Queen Square London WC1
Printed in Great Britain by
Whitstable Litho Whitstable
All rights reserved

All applications for performing rights should be
addressed to Clive Goodwin Associates, 79 Cromwell
Road, London SW7

British Library Cataloguing in Publication Data

Griffiths, Trevor
    All good men ; and, Absolute beginners.
    I. Title
    822'.9'14   PR6057.R52A/

    ISBN 0-571-10815-6

ALL GOOD MEN

All Good Men was first broadcast by BBC TV as a
Play for Today on 31 January 1974. The cast was as
follows:

EDWARD WAITE	Bill Fraser
RICHARD MASSINGHAM	Ronald Pickup
WILLIAM	Jack Shepherd
MARIA	Frances de la Tour
Script Editor	Ann Scott
Designer	Peter Brachacki
Producer	Graeme McDonald
Director	Michael Lindsay-Hogg

CHARACTERS

EDWARD WAITE: 70; Labour politician; born Manchester
      working class; life spent in trade union and labour
      movement.   Now lives in relative affluence in
      semi-retirement.

MARIA: 28; daughter of second marriage; teaches art in
      London comprehensive; married; separated.

WILLIAM: 23; son of second marriage; research post in
      history and sociology at University of Manchester.

RICHARD MASSINGHAM: 38; current affairs television
      producer; Winchester and Oxford.

MARY: Maid.

SETS: Conservatory, living room, dining room, hall and
      principal bedroom of Waite's country house in Surrey.

1. INT. CONSERVATORY. DAY

Conservatory of EDWARD WAITE's country house. Late
afternoon. Crisp sun.

The house is large but not opulent: twelve usable rooms,
good lawns front and back, and for this home counties
territory desirably remote.

WAITE sits in a comfortable wicker chair facing the sun.
He holds an open file on his knee, flicks a page from
time to time, mutters the occasional word or phrase out
loud.

He's old, seventy, grizzled, thick-necked, fleshy not
fat, hair cropped close to the scalp, yet somehow
miraculously parted on the left. He wears a white shirt,
red tie, gaberdine trousers with turnups, plaid slippers,
a brown woollen cardigan unbuttoned. On a table by his
left arm, a large pocket watch and a distinctive briar,
unfilled, on an ashtray. No pouch, no matches.

High shot. We see, ten feet from him, an Arriflex on a
tripod, facing him. He stares at it. On the floor,
unrigged, light battens, wiring, boards, lighting trunks
and other film production paraphernalia.

He looks back at his file.

WAITE: *(Quietly, as though to a question)* '26 was the
    turning point, I suppose ... You couldn't work in the
    pit as I did and not be affected. *(Pause)* Politically,
    I mean.

    (WAITE turns a page, sniffs. His voice is strong still,
    rather harsh, the jagged Manchester consonants still
    glinting in the oily wash of his received standard

English.

MASSINGHAM in from the house. Late 30s, thick-haired,
blond, supple. He wears an Italian suit of bottle
green thin corduroy, a splendid lacy shirt with full
collar open at the neck, built-up two-tone shoes in
black and brown. He returns easily to his seat
opposite WAITE's, in front of and beneath the camera;
picks up his clipboarded notes.)

MASSINGHAM: I'm sorry it took so long ...

WAITE: No no.

MASSINGHAM: Anyway, we're all fixed for tomorrow. Ten
o'clock. *(A hint of a question there.)*

WAITE: Ten o'clock.

MASSINGHAM: I think the garden stuff we've just done will
look good. It's a lovely house.
(Pause.
WAITE sucks on the empty pipe.)
I wouldn't have thought Surrey ... right, somehow,
given your life.

WAITE: No? No, perhaps not. *(Pause)* It's handy for
London. *(Smiling, rather pompous)* I *live* here. They
haven't buried me yet.
(MASSINGHAM shares the smile, a managed deference
neatly glossing his arrogance. Silence, as he checks
his notes.)

MASSINGHAM: It's very kind of you to ask me to stay. It
will help. *(Pause)* I hope we'll ... count ourselves
friends when it's over.

WAITE: *(Grinning)* As long as you don't mind a row or two.
I've never managed to last very long without a
flaming good row.

MASSINGHAM: Why not. It's what the history's about
anyway, isn't it. Put a bit of life in the old archive.

WAITE: *(Checking watch)* Dinner's at seven. I can't last longer than seven. Never could.

MASSINGHAM: Ah. Would you mind if I didn't this evening? I usually have dinner with the crew the first evening. It's ... er ... a sort of ritual.

WAITE: I quite understand. Happen you'll need a key. There's usually one on the coatstand thing in the hall.

MASSINGHAM: Thank you. *(Pause. Picks up case.)* Well, would you like a short canter over the early ground? But let's make sure we don't spoil tomorrow's spontaneity.

WAITE: Whatever you say.

MASSINGHAM: Just to get the feel and the range for tomorrow. *(Pause)* By the way, if you don't mind I'd like to call you *Lord* Waite, if that's all right. *(Smiling)* There's no chance of your not accepting is there?...

WAITE: None at all. *(Pause)* There must be no leak, of course.

MASSINGHAM: That's understood. You see my point, don't you? By the time all this is in the can and edited, the New Year's Honours List will have come and gone and I don't want to end up with egg on my face. *(Making note on pad)* So: Lord Waite. *(Pause)* Tell us something about your early life. You were born in Manchester, weren't you. Well, your parents were Manchester people and you were born in Manchester, one of seven children in 1903. What was it like?

WAITE: *Six*, six children.

MASSINGHAM: *(Amending)* I'm sorry.

(A little hold up)

WAITE: Do you want me to answer?

MASSINGHAM: Please.

*(WAITE assuming stiffish interview role at once, or
merely politician's role.)*

WAITE: They were bad times, those were. My God, but they
were bad. It's hard to conceive, now, from here,
how ... viciously working people were exploited in
those days. Eight of us, mother, father, four lads,
two lasses, in four rooms, two up, two down,
lavatory in the yard at the back. Beswick in
Manchester we lived, 14 Milton Street. Dad worked as
a labourer at Bradford colliery. Brought home
eighteen bob a week. Don't ask how we managed ...

MASSINGHAM: I think this part of the story is terribly
important and ... I'm keen to get the flavour
absolutely right. Was it all bad, for example?

WAITE: No no. We were *alive*, for one thing. That was
something. *(Pause)* And ... we had each other. Down
the street, up the street, round the corner, down the
next one. We were all in the same boat. *Bound* to
each other, you might say. Aunts and uncles and
cousins and ... just neighbours. *(Pause)* There
mightn't have been much hope around, but there wasn't
too much despair either.

MASSINGHAM: What about schooling?

WAITE: Schooling? Nasty, brutish and short is the
phrase that comes to mind. I organised the first
monitors' strike: 1912 that'd be.

MASSINGHAM: Oh, on what issue?

WAITE: I thought monitors should be paid. Some days
we'd do more work than the teachers.

MASSINGHAM: What happened?

WAITE: We got a belting. Sixteen of us. Headmistress
took us all into the hall, leathered us till we could
hardly stand, then forced us to confess the error of

12

our ways before the whole school.

MASSINGHAM: Did you do it?

WAITE: Yes. When I saw there was nothing else for it.
She'd put the fear of God up the others. There was
no point in going it alone. *(Smiling)* So I recanted:
lived to fight another day, you might say.

(MASSINGHAM picks up WAITE's book.)

MASSINGHAM: Is that in the book? I can't remember it
at all.

WAITE: *(Slowly)* I don't think it is. It's a long thing,
is a life. A book can't hold it all.

(Pause)

MASSINGHAM: Of course.

(Puts book down and makes brief notes.)

What else do you remember? About the early days.

WAITE: Everything, bloody near. Should I say that?

(MASSINGHAM smiles him on.)

It's what fed my politics right through my life.
(Pause) We might've been living on another planet
for all anyone cared. *(Pause)* I remember. *(Pause)* Hot
summer nights I'd sit on the front doorstep and
just ... listen ... to the street. You could learn
more about a community then - about its hopes and
fears, its desperation and its courage - in one
night on the fronts than any amount of erudite
'sociological' investigation could tell you now.
(Pause) The pavement was made of big smooth stone
slabs, that big, bigger, bedded in soil, you know.
And between each slab and the next, a little ripple of
moss, dark green, soft as velvet. I used to ... I
used to ... peel it ... upwards ... with my finger,
see how long a strip I could manage before it broke.
And then I'd take it in my hands and smell it. Close

my eyes and smell it. And ... imagine ... whole ...
landscapes filled with ... growing things. *(Pause)*
And ... I can hear it now ... eyes closed, smelling
the moss and the earth clinging to it ... there'd be
the *crack, crack, crack* of shoe heels on bedroom
walls ... pulverising bedbugs gone crazy in the heat.
(He grins suddenly, relishing the tale.
MASSINGHAM makes a note on the pad.)

The good old days.

MASSINGHAM: And the war?

(Silence. It's darkening a little.)

WAITE: And the war.

MASSINGHAM: *(Silky)* Just in time, some people have said.

WAITE: In time for what?

MASSINGHAM: In time, somebody said, I can't recall who,
'In time to lance the boil of social unrest'. Ireland,
women, industrial ferment, syndicalism. That's the
theory, anyway ...

WAITE: Ah, the theory.

(There is in WAITE, and MASSINGHAM senses it, a
reluctance to talk about the war.

WAITE begins searching through his file.)

MASSINGHAM: Well, I'm sure we can look at it later on if
you'd ...

WAITE: *(Decides to talk)* I was eleven. Just. Dad was
thirty-eight, thirty-nine. Volunteered the first
week of the war. Joe and Philip followed him.
Nineteen and seventeen. All dead by Christmas. Joe
had both legs blown off by a shell. Philip and Dad
died charging machine guns. *(Pause)* I've still got
this *(Tapping file.)* letter. *(Clears throat, reading.)*
'You are leaving home to fight for the safety and
honour of my Empire. Belgium, whose country we are

pledged to defend, has been attacked and France is about to be invaded by the same powerful foe. I have implicit confidence in you my soldiers. Duty is your watchword, and I know your duty will be nobly done. I shall follow your every movement with deepest interest and mark with eager satisfaction your daily progress. Indeed, your welfare will never be absent from my thoughts. I pray God to bless you and guard you and bring you back victorious. Signed, George V, by the Grace of God King and Emperor, this day, August 12th, 1914.' *(Pause)* The telegrams announcing the deaths were ... more succinct. I think my mother burnt them. At any rate, they're not there. There she is.

(Hands photo of mother to MASSINGHAM, he hands it back.)

MASSINGHAM: It must have hit you pretty hard ... your father ... and brothers.

WAITE: That's right. Me and a few million others. Bleak. At least I can remember him whole. You know, intact. For ten years after the war ended you couldn't leave the house without bumping into someone you used to know when he had two legs or arms.

MASSINGHAM: So how important would you say the Great War was to your political development?

WAITE: *(Sombre)* You could say ... it made a man of me ... *(Pause)* I left school on my thirteenth birthday. Went down the pit. That's how I came to be involved in the trade union movement. *(Pause)* It was suddenly all very clear to me. As I put it in my book, a Pauline revelation: if my people were going to get anywhere, they'd have to get there by Shank's, there'd be nobody giving them a lift.

MASSINGHAM: *(Checking file)* And ... you joined the Labour

Party, what, in the twenties sometime ...

WAITE: ILP first. That was the Labour Party where I came from. Then the Labour Party proper, after '24 and the minority government.

MASSINGHAM: Did you ever imagine then, in those early, distant days, that you might achieve what you have achieved, in the years that followed?

WAITE: Oh yes. Oh yes. *(Pause)* You see, we were *right*. *(Pause)* There's nothing you can't do, if you're right.

MASSINGHAM: *(Simply)* Nothing? *(Silence)*

WAITE: *(Levelly)* That's right. Always provided it's possible.

(The conservatory lights go on suddenly. The MAID stands in the doorway.)

What is it, Mary?

MARY: Six-thirty, sir.

WAITE: Yes, thank you, Mary.

(She takes tea things, and leaves.
MASSINGHAM puts his clipboard down into a small black attache case, which he fastens and locks.)

MASSINGHAM: I fancy that could make one section on its own. I want to put a picture researcher on it. It has a nice feel. Would you happen to know whether that pre-1914 environment still stands?

WAITE: No, I wouldn't *happen* to know, young man. I made it my *business* to know. And I can tell you it doesn't. We saw it off; rooted it up; and thousands like it. *(Pause)* Part of our history.

MASSINGHAM: Of course. Forgive me.

WAITE: I s'll have to get ready for dinner.

MASSINGHAM: And I'll drive down to the village to see the crew. *(On his feet.)* Thank you. It's going to be marvellous.

WAITE: *(Drily)* It's a good story. *(Pause)* Don't forget
    your key.
MASSINGHAM: No. I'm extremely grateful for all your
    time and trouble. I'll see you tomorrow then.
    (MASSINGHAM leaves.
    WAITE sits on, tired suddenly. He stares straight
    ahead, empty pipe in hand.)

2. INT. BEDROOM. NIGHT

WAITE stands in front of wardrobe mirror, fastening his
front collar-stud. The same red tie. Dark suit jacket.
The room is large, airy. He crosses to the dressing
table, swallows two tablets with a glass of water laid
out for him there on a tray.
He takes in the framed photographs of his second wife,
ANN, his daughter MARIA on her wedding day, his son
WILLIAM at graduation, his mother around 35, dressed in
black blouse and skirt, short steel-coloured hair,
rimless spectacles.
He picks this last frame up, studies it, puts it down,
crosses to the leaded windows, stares out on to the lit
drive, picks up a pair of binoculars from the window seat,
attempts to pierce the blackness with them, fails,
finding only his own broken reflection in the window
panes. Over this image, the voice of Ramsay Macdonald
announces his intention to seek George V's permission to
form a national government.

3. INT. DINING ROOM. NIGHT

WAITE sits in the light at the top of the long table, the
rest of the room shadowed.

WAITE stares at the vichyssoise, puts a spoon in,
retrieves it, lets it rest in the bowl.
L.S. He stares straight ahead, teeming with voices. Slow
track, zoom, to B.C.U. Chamberlain's Croydon Peace with
Honour, Attlee pledging 'responsible government' in 1945,
Bevin's 'naked into the conference chamber' speech,
Gaitskell's 'we will fight, fight and fight again to save
the party we love'. The cheers and counter-cheers cover
his stiff, sweating face in C.U. Silence. His wife's
voice, in half-whisper, mock-cold, ironic and contemptuous.
ANN: *(V.O.)* Maybe you'd better kiss me then. Go on. Get
     down and *kiss* me ...

     (A sharp, delicate spasm. His head slumps forward,
     catches the edge of the bowl, tilting soup into his
     frozen face.)

     (V.O., very distant) Isn't that what you want ...

4.   INT.   HALL.   NIGHT

Hall clock shows 12.15. Light from the living room, hall
darkish. MASSINGHAM lets himself in by the front door,
returns the key to the hallstand drawer, is pulled by the
light, moves into the living room.

5.   INT.   LIVING ROOM.   NIGHT

MARIA WAITE, 28, stocky like her father, dark, almost
gypsyish, sits on the settee flicking a New Statesman.
She holds a half-filled glass of something in her hand.
She wears trousers, boots, thigh-length cotton smock.
Sees MASSINGHAM, who has stopped just inside the doorway.
MARIA: Richard Massingham.
MASSINGHAM: Yes ...

18

MARIA: *(Standing)* Maria ... Waite.

MASSINGHAM: Ah.

MARIA: Won't you come in?

MASSINGHAM: *(Frowning)* Thank you. Erm ...

MARIA: Can I get you a drink?

MASSINGHAM: Thanks.

    (She stops by the cabinet, waiting.)

    Scotch. Thank you.

MARIA: *(Pouring)* My father's ...

    (Inching up the glass with studied precision.)

    ... had some sort of ... heart attack.

MASSINGHAM: What?

MARIA: *(Bringing drink)* Or perhaps merely a serious bout
    of indigestion ... Sit down, won't you ... The
    doctor can't make his mind up.

MASSINGHAM: *(Sitting, rather heavily)* I see. *(MARIA
    resumes her seat.)* I'm ... sorry. *(MARIA ignores this.)*
    Have they ... taken him in?

MARIA: No. They've left a nurse.

    (As though savouring a recent quotation.)

    He has a history of hypertension, but if it was a
    coronary it appears to have been a relatively minor
    one. As far as one can tell.

MASSINGHAM: I see.

MARIA: We'll know in the morning. When the results of
    the tests are through.

MASSINGHAM: How ... how is he?

MARIA: Would you believe 'comfortable'? Floating on a
    sea of morphine and anti-coagulants is probably more
    accurate but decidedly less reassuring. *(Pause)* You
    didn't mean that, though, did you.

MASSINGHAM: *(A tactical incomprehension)* I'm sorry ...

MARIA: *(Bluntly)* He'll have to rest. *(Pause)* But he won't die. Not this time. *(Standing)* Another?

MASSINGHAM: *(Showing glass)* Thank you, no.

(MARIA crosses to the cabinet, pours herself another scotch.)

(Suddenly) Would you mind if I used the phone?

MARIA: Help yourself.

(MASSINGHAM looks round the room. MARIA points it out. He crosses, taking a small black address book out of his pocket, stops, looks in her direction. She catches the look. Unyieldingly.)

Would you like me to leave?

MASSINGHAM: No no. Please.

(MASSINGHAM dials the number. MARIA returns to her seat, back to him, picks up the New Statesman *again.)*

(Phone) Room 8, please.

(MASSINGHAM waits, looks in MARIA's direction.)

Eddie, Richard. Hi. Look, sorry to call you at this hour. What? No, no. Look, Mr ... Waite has been taken ill. Yes. No, it's not clear how ill at the moment, but it's obviously going to be a few days at the very least. Ahunh. Ahunh. No, I want to use the time picking up background footage. Manchester. I'll give you the details when you collect your gear in the morning. *(Pause)* I know that, Eddie, and I'll authorise it. Eddie, I know that. All right, you travel up, that's a day, you shoot, day and a half, maybe two, travel back, no problem. *(Pause)* So take it from Jeannie's float. *(Pause)* In writing. You'll have it. *(Pause)* Well, general stuff. There's an area he was born in, he claims has been pulled down and rebuilt. I want you to check it out, shoot what's there, whatever it is, old or new, we can use either, same slums or new ones, towerblock variety. And there

20

may be a couple of interviews with people who knew
him in those days, I'll get the researcher on to that
first thing in the morning and let you know. No,
there's no angle, save maybe a news angle, who knows.
Be prepared, eh? *(Pause)* All right, we'll talk in the
morning. Thanks, Eddie.

*(Phone down, he's back in the room. Crosses to the
cabinet, pours himself another drink.)*

Would you mind if I ...?

(MASSINGHAM gestures at his chair.)

MARIA: Be my guest.

(MASSINGHAM sits down. They face each other. Silence.)

MASSINGHAM: Is it simply distress ... or have I offended
you in some way, Mrs Bryant?

MARIA: My, but you boys do your homework, don't you?

MASSINGHAM: Well?

MARIA: Don't ... patronise me, Mr Massingham.

MASSINGHAM: I'm sorry. I didn't mean to.

(Silence. The question lingers.)

MARIA: I can't decide whether your sensitivity is real
or tactical.

MASSINGHAM: Ah.

MARIA: There you go again. Ah. Poor suffering *inferior*
creature. Ah. *(Pause)* He's old and he's tired and
he's sick. Leave him be.

MASSINGHAM: Is that what he wants?

MARIA: No. It's what I want.

MASSINGHAM: He's a public man. A great one, some would
say.

MARIA: What would *you* say?

MASSINGHAM: That's not my brief. I present; others
judge.

MARIA: Ah.

MASSINGHAM: Ah?

(A brief smile between them.)

MARIA: Tell me about your ... brief.

MASSINGHAM: *(Cleanly)* I'm setting up a series called
'Living History'. Long hard-core interviews with
living figures who embody important strands in our
relatively recent past. This is the pilot. The
first. They buy or reject this one.

MARIA: Why my father?

MASSINGHAM: I wrote to ten professors of politics, ten
professors of modern history, outlined my brief, and
asked them to list the people they considered best
fitted it. Your father was mentioned twelve times.
A major trade union leader, a quarter of a century in
the Commons, three Cabinet posts, party treasurer,
party chairman ...

MARIA: Man of the people.

MASSINGHAM: As you say.

MARIA: What about *you*?

MASSINGHAM: What about me? I'm not important.

MARIA: Too bright for Eton. Marlborough?

MASSINGHAM: Winchester.

MARIA: Yes. I should have recognised that distinctive
'I'm not important' style of arrogance.

MASSINGHAM: It's amazing. You're exactly the way I
expected your father might be.

MARIA: Don't tell me. It's chip on the shoulder time.
You're all the bloody same. The minute your sleek
charm fails to make the requisite impression, you fall
to whining about chips on the shoulder. *(Pause)* Your
dispensation isn't *natural*, you know. Or God-given.
It's bred. Like my resistance. I thought they'd've
told you that, while they were ... making you.

(MASSINGHAM stands, smiles, just a touch uncertain
before the ironic onslaught.)

MASSINGHAM: I think I'll go to bed. I - er - I'd prefer
not to fight, if it's all the same with you.

MARIA: Especially with someone who insists on hitting
below the intellect. I know what you mean.

MASSINGHAM: Will you ... stay?

(MARIA gets up, wanders to cabinet.)

MARIA: A few days. Until he's on his feet. Term's
ended. I teach. Oh, I suppose you've 'had your
researcher' on that too. Did she tell you I'd left
my husband?

MASSINGHAM: Good night, Mrs Bryant.

(He leaves the room, very calm, slightly steely,
reassured by the late show of vulnerability in her.
MARIA watches him out, pours another drink, stares up
at the picture of the '45 Labour government on the
wall, her father four seats to the right of Clement
Attlee.)

6. INT. HALL. DAY

A battered grip, raincoat across it, in the hall.

7. INT. WAITE'S BEDROOM. DAY

Curtained. WILLIAM WAITE, twenty-three, stands at the
foot of the bed, staring at WAITE's sleeping face on the
pillow.

WILLIAM is of middle height, brown longish hair, untidy,
unkempt, with about four days growth of beard on his face.
He stands now, hands deep in pockets of olive green
combat coat, dispassionately watching his father, touches

of anger and contempt nudging the unconcern from time to time.

WAITE's eyes open. He focuses on WILLIAM.

WAITE: William?

WILLIAM: Rest.

    (WAITE's eyes close. Open.)

WAITE: Is your mother here?

WILLIAM: No.

8. INT. DINING ROOM. DAY

Lunch ending. Fruit.

WILLIAM and MASSINGHAM sit opposite each other in silence.
MARIA's half-eaten meal remains at the top of the table.
Voices in the hall.

Front door closing.

Car starting up.

MARIA in.

MARIA removes her plate and pours herself coffee.

MARIA: Christ, he's older and iller than father. Never
    stopped coughing the whole time we were up there.

MASSINGHAM: *(Handing bowl)* Fruit?

MARIA: No thanks.

WILLIAM: What's he got to say?

MARIA: Up Friday for an hour. No repeat this time, they
    think. Looks as if you'll get your programme after
    all, Mr Massingham.

    (MASSINGHAM smiles coolly.)

    Have you seen anything of mother?

WILLIAM: No.

MARIA: *(Quiet, excluding MASSINGHAM)* I had a letter about
    a month ago. From Estoril.

WILLIAM: Yeah. Where's that?

MARIA: Portugal.

WILLIAM: *(Characteristically terse, bitter)*   Jesus.

   (Long pause.) How is she?

MARIA: All right.   She's left Frederick.   Do you
   remember Frederick, the one with the teeth?

WILLIAM: Who was the marina developer?

MARIA: Frederick.   That was Frederick.   She's left him.

WILLIAM: Yeah?

   (Silence)

MARIA: She asked for your address.

WILLIAM: *(Standing)*   What about a drink?   Mr Massingham?

MASSINGHAM: Thank you, no.   I have some work to do.

WILLIAM: *(Pouring at drinks table)*   In this ... new ...
   golden age of unemployment it's difficult to know
   whether you are boasting or merely stating a fact.
   (Smiles bleakly at MASSINGHAM.)

   Sister?

MARIA: What is there?

WILLIAM: Sweet: Benedictine, Curacao, Drambuie.   Dry:
   Brandy, Calvados ... Canadian Ginger.   He must have
   had his Christmas present early from his friends in
   the City.   They *say* he used to like a glass of stout,
   in the old days. *(To MARIA.)* Yes?

MARIA: Brandy.   Stop making speeches.

WILLIAM: *(Pouring)*   What do you think of my father,
   Mr Massingham?

MASSINGHAM: *(Equable, guarded)*   I think he's a remarkable man.

MARIA: William.

WILLIAM: *(Fetching drinks to table)*   Remarkable.   Yes.   And
   the programme you're doing is, what, 'Living History',
   that's the title?

MASSINGHAM: Working title.

WILLIAM: Oh.   You might ... change it, you mean.

MASSINGHAM: It might be changed. Producers don't usually
        have the final say in series titles.

WILLIAM: So it could end up as ... 'Historical
        Curiosities' or ... 'Anomalies of History' ... or 'A
        Gallery of Class Traitors', mm?

MASSINGHAM: I think it a ... little unlikely.

WILLIAM: Do you. *(Pause)* I personally wouldn't mind in
        the least, you understand. Conceivably *he* might,
        though.

MASSINGHAM: *(Dry)* I believe I've already had the next
        speech from your sister.

WILLIAM: You think so?

        *(They stare at each other levelly. The absence of
        empathy is palpable.)*

MARIA: I saw a book in Compendium the other day called
        The Knee of Listening. I couldn't believe it. I'm
        sure it's been planted by somebody making a detailed
        study of the double take. Mine was monumental.
        (Silence.

        MASSINGHAM smiles civilly in MARIA's direction.)

MASSINGHAM: *(To MARIA)* Would it be convenient to call in
        for a chat with your father now, do you think?

MARIA: Ten minutes. You mustn't tire him.

MASSINGHAM: *(Draining coffee)* Good.

WILLIAM: You haven't really said anything, have you?

MASSINGHAM: What do you want? Where I was born, early
        life, parents, school, relationships? What purpose
        would it serve, except to confirm your view that,
        unlike you presumably, I'm a total product of my
        environment.

WILLIAM: *(Gently)* I meant more the programme. *(Pause)*
        I mean, you're too intelligent, too clever, really to
        believe that you can talk as it were neutrally about

the past. So, when you choose to examine the social
and political history of twentieth-century Britain
through the eyes and mouth of a major Labour
politician, you must have some ... framework ... some
point of view, attitude, mm? ... to hold the thing
together.

MASSINGHAM: I don't see why.

WILLIAM: *(Gently almost)* But that would mean ... you
didn't *care*. You were indifferent.

MASSINGHAM: The conventional rules of biography and
historiography will be observed. I can't see that it
makes better history if one has an axe to grind.

WILLIAM: Can't you? You see - and I work in the margins
of history and sociology currently, and have reason to
look at the matter fairly closely - you can't look at
a mainstream representative of Labourism in this
century - my father, say - *without declaring an
interest*. Because Labourism is itself a critique:
both of extra-parliamentary revolutionism on the one
hand and of parliamentary toryism on the other. In
other words, it's not a *state*, describable, with
planes and surfaces and textures. Or at least, it's
not in essence that. It's basically a *process*, a
more or less dynamic interaction between value and
value, assertion and counter-assertion, stimulus and
response. You can't just ... describe the 'Welfare
State', you have to ... account for it. And that
means, inevitably, making some assessment of its
'goodness' or whatever, of its preferability to what
it superseded; and of its deficiencies in terms of
what was *actually realisable, potent*, in the period
during which it was being constructed.

MASSINGHAM: I don't disagree. But I'm not writing the

history. Your father is. Because he has lived it.
I'm simply the film camera, the tape recorder, the
lighting man ...

WILLIAM: The programme controller. The film editor. The
picture researcher. The sound mixer. The blurb
writer. The audience softener. *(Pause)* It's not
even *that*. *(Pause)* Suppose it's the North American
Indians you want to talk about. Now. How do you set
about writing a history of the red Indian in the
nineteenth century or in this without mentioning the
word genocide? Yet merely to invoke the concept is
to begin to develop a critique of American society and
the economic 'necessities' of contemporary capitalism.
Your answer - superficially attractive - is presumably
to invite an Indian chief to tell it 'how it was'.
Some Edward Waite of the Nez Percé or Arapahoe, mm?
The question still remains, which chief? Spotted
Tail? Geronimo? Because most of them *led* their
people into obliteration. *Objectively*, most of them
sold out, assimilated, *settled* for ignominy,
starvation, slow death on remote and barren
reservations, in face of the 'higher technology'. Yet
Geronimo and others proved that objectively another
way was open to the Indian, based on attritional
struggle, organisation, discipline, courage and will.
If you want to write the history, you have to say who
was right, Mr Massingham. You have to *choose* your
spokesman.

MASSINGHAM: The analogy is peculiarly unapt, if I may say
so. The history of your father's 'people', if I
might put it that way, has been the history of
increasing control over their social and work
environment and the steady amelioration of the quality

of life; and your father's leading role in this
'progress' I would take to be pretty well self-evident.

WILLIAM: A value. At last. *(Pause)* Let me tell you how I
see my father's role. If this coronary had killed
him, I'd've suggested an epitaph from a speech from
Kicking Bird, chief of the Kiowas, who said, towards
the end of his highly distinguished life, all there is
to be said about my father's sort of leadership: 'I
long ago took the white man by the hand; I have never
let it go; I have held it with a strong and firm
grasp. I have worked hard to bring my people on the
white man's road. Sometimes I have been compelled to
work with my back towards the white people so that
they have not seen my face, and they may have thought
I was working against them; but I have worked with one
heart and one object. I have looked ahead to the
future and have worked for the children of my people,
to bring them into a position that, when they become
men and women, they will take up the white road.
(Pause) But now I am as a stone, broken and thrown
away. And I fear most that my people will go back to
the old road.'
(Silence. MARIA stands deliberately, leaves.
MASSINGHAM stares at WILLIAM.)

MASSINGHAM: *(Coolly)* So you hate your father.

WILLIAM: *(Laughing tightly)* You listen but you don't
hear, Mr Massingham.
(WILLIAM stands, leaves.)

9. INT. CONSERVATORY. DAY

Conservatory. Dullish afternoon.

WAITE AND MARIA play cribbage on a small card table.
WAITE sits in a bathchair, wears pyjamas and thick plaid
dressing gown. A car rug covers legs and feet.
MARIA deals six cards, they carefully discard two apiece
into the box, he cuts the pack, she turns up a jack,
smiles.

WAITE: Lucky at cards ...

> *(WAITE plays a seven, MARIA scores with an eight,*
> *they play out. He calls three. She shows seven, has*
> *six in the box.)*

MARIA: *(Moving matchstick)* Dead hole.

WAITE: All right. I'll give it you.

> *(MARIA smiles ironically at the board. He's only*
> *just turned the corner.)*

MARIA: Sure?

WAITE: Don't be cheeky.

MARIA: *(Collecting cards)* Not like you to give up.

WAITE: Rubbish. When I know I'm licked, there's nobody
gives up faster. There's no joy to be had fighting
losing battles. How much is that?

MARIA: 30p.

WAITE: You'll have to wait.

> *(MARIA places the pack on the board.)*

MARIA: Are you warm enough?

WAITE: I'm fine. Don't fuss.

MARIA: Do you want anything?

WAITE: No. I'll go back up in a minute. I feel tired.

MARIA: You look fine.

WAITE: I feel all right. I feel better than I did before
I had it. Just a bit tired, that's all.

> *(Pause.*

30

*MARIA stands, walks over to the windows, looks out
down the long lawns.
WAITE puts his hand out, touches a long, brown
cardboard box on a table to the right. Looks at
MARIA. Removes the hand.)*

MARIA: *(Back still to window)* Have you had a chat with
William yet?

WAITE: I've never had a *chat* with William in my life.
You can have a fight with him, or a flaming great row,
or you can make the occasional interruption to his
speeches. Chat, no.
*(MARIA scratches a stain from the window pane.
Longish pause.)*
We exchanged ... unpleasantries this morning. Very
briefly. Why?

MARIA: He's upset about something. I don't know ...

WAITE: Isn't he always? Vietnam, Cambodia, Industrial
Relations, Wounded ... Knee, was it? How else should
he be, a lad of mine?

MARIA: Maybe.
(Pause)
He used to cry for you, when you had all-night sittings
and didn't come home. A long time ago.

WAITE: Day before yesterday.
(Pause)
How's school?

MARIA: School ... is school. I don't want to talk about
it.

WAITE: I thought you liked teaching. Fine big
comprehensive, airy classrooms, lots of equipment ...

MARIA: Yeah.
*(Silence.
She smokes a cigarette, tense.)*

WAITE: My day, it was something different.

MARIA: *(Terse)*   Yes, I know about that, Dad ...

   (Silence)

WAITE: *(Tentative)*   Do you see anything of your husband?

MARIA: I had a letter from him, while ago. He wants to
   re-marry. An actress.

WAITE: And you?

MARIA: Once is enough for me.

WAITE: Are you sure? It's a long time.

MARIA: *(Bluntly, turning)*   My needs are relatively few
   and ... not difficult to satisfy.

   (WAITE looks away, embarrassed, an old Puritan.)

   I have an address for mother, if you'd like me to
   write.

WAITE: *(Studying a* Guardian *he's picked up)*   What about?

   (MARIA doesn't answer.

   *After a moment, WAITE looks over the top of the paper
   at her.*

   MASSINGHAM in, in good, short topcoat, carrying grip.)

MASSINGHAM: *(Approaching)*   Forgive me, I'm just off.

WAITE: Have a safe trip.

MASSINGHAM: Thank you. I've ... I've made arrangements
   for the crew to arrive Monday morning, as agreed. Are
   you sure you'll feel up to it?

WAITE: Yes yes. They'll have to cut me up in pieces and
   feed me to the dogs before they'll be shot of me,
   don't you fret.

MASSINGHAM: Fine. Fine. Well ... *(Moving)* Oh, would
   you mind if I came back Sunday evening, just to get
   things set up?

WAITE: Come back whenever you like. It's no bother.

MARIA: Sunday's your birthday.

WAITE: So it is. *(To MASSINGHAM.)* If you get back soon

32

enough, you'll be in time for the jelly and a piece of cake.

MASSINGHAM: Are you sure ... I wouldn't want to intrude on a family ...

WAITE: Go on with you. We've never been what you'd call struck on birthdays in our family. We'll see you Sunday dinner.

MASSINGHAM: Thank you. Goodbye.

(MASSINGHAM leaves. MARIA's distaste is fairly patent.)

WAITE: Nice feller. *(Musing)* Do you know, I can't remember if he's BBC or the other lot.

MARIA: Does it matter?

WAITE: No. I shouldn't think so.

(MARIA stubs her cigarette out on an ashtray by the brown cardboard box.)

MARIA: I think I might push off home, if you're going to be all right.

WAITE: *(Taking her hand)* Do I have to be dying to get a bit of attention then?

MARIA: *(Carefully disengaging)* Don't be silly.

WAITE: What is it?

MARIA: Nothing. I don't like that man, that's all. I don't trust him. I don't think *you* should.

WAITE: Oh. I see. *That*'s how you suck eggs. Well, I'd never have thought it.

(MARIA stares hard at WAITE, frowning.)

And what makes you think I trust him?

MARIA: How do you mean?

WAITE: Listen, baby. I've been in this game a long while. You don't get where I got by trusting people. And especially not the likes of him.

MARIA: He's clever.

WAITE: *(Unconvinced)* Is he?

MARIA: And he doesn't care. About you, I mean.

WAITE: He doesn't have to. It's a free country. *(Pause)* All right? *(Pause)* I don't understand you young people. I don't. The minute you feel something you think your only responsibility is to express it. Now, in my line of business that's tantamount to suicide. Shout when you have to, smile when you don't, Keir Hardie used to say. Mmm?

(Silence)

MARIA: Hadn't you better rest?

WAITE: Sit down a minute, will you. There's something I want to ask of you.

(MARIA sits carefully. WAITE draws the brown box laboriously on to his knee, breathing a little at the exertion. Looks at her. Removes the lid. Tilts it in her direction. She inspects the contents, puzzled.) Robes. They've just come from the tailors. I've accepted a peerage. It'll be announced in the New Year's Honours List. You're to tell no one. I wanted you to know.

(Long silence. MARIA stares at the robes.)

Say something.

MARIA: Say what? *(Pause)* Why?

WAITE: Why not? I wasn't made for retirement and obscurity. I'm no ... thinker, I need to be doing. *(Pause)* It's an arena. What's wrong with that?

MARIA: How? The *Tories* put you up for it?

WAITE: It's a technicality. A deal. I was offered in 1970 but I thought I might get a safe seat in a bye-election. *(Pause)* I'll take the Labour whip. It's perfectly normal.

(MARIA looks at the robes again, back at WAITE.)

MARIA: *(Finally)* So do it.

34

WAITE: I need your help.

MARIA: *(Slightly numb)* Yes?

WAITE: There's an investiture ceremony in February
         sometime at the Palace. *(Pause)* Now that your mother's
         finally ... *(Long pause)* I'd like you to ... accompany
         me. Be my ... woman. If you would.
         *(They look at each other for a long time. MARIA is
         finally distracted by the sound of whistling from the
         garden. She looks out, stands, takes the brown box,
         deftly lids it, places it on the table. WILLIAM in
         from the garden.
         WILLIAM stops, surveys the scene, his lips pursed,
         the whistling gone silent.)*

WILLIAM: *(Finally)* The squirrels are killing that yew.
         You should have someone take a gun to them.
         *(WILLIAM moves on into the house.
         WAITE looks at MARIA, who's fiddling abstractedly with
         the box's securing tapes.)*

WAITE: I can't understand a word he says, you know. How
         can a squirrel kill a tree? Mmm?

MARIA: They eat the bark. When the stripped parts meet
         in a circle, the tree dies.
         (Long silence. WAITE ponders it, very pale, tired, old.)
         Let's get you inside.
         *(WAITE lets himself be hauled up, shuffles slowly
         towards the doorway using MARIA as a crutch. They
         reach the conservatory doorway. He stops, points to
         the box, hangs on to the french window as MARIA gathers
         it. She returns to help him.)*

WAITE: You didn't answer.

MARIA: We'll talk. Come.
         (MARIA helps WAITE into the house.)

10. INT. LIVING ROOM. NIGHT

Living room. Night, around 7.45. Some subdued talk, clink
of glasses, crockery, from adjoining dining room. MARY in,
carrying a birthday cake, which she places on the coffee
table before lighting the single candle. We see the pink
iced message: EDUCATE AGITATE ORGANISE. HAPPY BIRTHDAY
DAD, *in the style of a William Morris SDF banner. MARY*
takes a knife from her apron, places it on the plate,
crosses to the half-open dining room door, stands until
she catches MARIA's eye, nods, leaves.

11. INT. DINING ROOM. NIGHT

Dining room. MARIA, WAITE, MASSINGHAM. WAITE wears a
suit, looks stronger though not fully recovered.
MARIA: One drink, the doctor said. What will it be?
WAITE: *(Pointing to wine)* Some of that'll do.

    (MARIA pours him half a glass, hands the bottle round.)
MARIA: Now bring your glasses through. There's a surprise
    (MARIA takes her father's arm, leads them off into
    the living room.)

12. INT. LIVING ROOM. NIGHT

WAITE: *(Walking carefully)* All the world's a classroom
    to this one. Born organiser. Do this, do that ...
MARIA: *(Squeezing his arm)* Go on ...

    (They reach the coffee table, MASSINGHAM some steps
    behind. WAITE sees the cake. Stares, moved. Smiles.
    Approaches. Reads the inscription. Turns to MARIA.
    Looks at her.)
    Happy birthday!
    (WAITE doesn't speak. Looks back at the cake.)

WAITE: S'elp me God.

MARIA: Do you need any help?

(WAITE bends carefully, blows out the candle.)

WAITE: Isn't that something!

MARIA: Shall I cut it or will you?

(WAITE sits down, faces it, staring still.)

WAITE: No no. I want a picture of that before it's
destroyed. Do you mind?

MARIA: *(Laughing)* Not in the least. It'll probably
taste terrible.

MASSINGHAM: May I look?

(WAITE gestures MASSINGHAM in. He studies it.
WILLIAM in from hall, in outdoor clothes. He carries
a small package.
Studies the group.)

It's marvellous. Where's it from?

MARIA: I took it from a William Morris banner. You
should see the original.

MASSINGHAM: Marvellous. Is that what you teach,
domestic science?

MARIA: I teach art.

(MARIA sees WILLIAM in the doorway.)

You made it then.

WILLIAM: Yeah, I got stuck at Guildford coming back.
(To WAITE) Sorry I missed your ... thing.

WAITE: *(Slight brusqueness)* Come in. Get yourself a
drink.

WILLIAM: *(To cabinet)* Anybody else?

(They indicate full glasses, settle down.
WILLIAM joins them with his glass. Approaches his
father.)

I bought you this.

(Hands WAITE parcel. Stares at cake.)

WAITE: Very kind of you.

(A moment's hesitation. Begins to open it. WILLIAM's eyes move from the cake to MARIA, who's watching him closely, slightly apprehensive. He smiles tightly. WAITE holds up a book.)

Indian ... Oratory. (Pause. Looks at WILLIAM.) Will I find this ... instructive?

WILLIAM: You might. Tell me when you've read it.

WAITE: I will. I will. Thank you. *(Pause)* Maria bought me the tie.

(WAITE pulls the tails of it from his breast to show WILLIAM.)

And ... I had a ... *(Searches for it on the settee where he sits, finds it.)* ... a very expensive tin of tobacco from Mr Massingham. See.

(WILLIAM looks at MARIA, back at tobacco.)

WILLIAM: Tobacco.

WAITE: That's right.

WILLIAM: Mmm.

(WILLIAM takes a sip from his glass.)

Very nice.

MASSINGHAM: *(Standing)* I ... got you something else, I don't know if it'll be of any use.

(MASSINGHAM crosses to a chair by the door, takes up a canvas picture folder, unties the laces, takes out a sort of large black album, brings it over to the settee, sits down by WAITE.)

It's work as well, but I thought you might just like to have it for your own use afterwards. *(He begins flicking the pages.)* I've had a picture researcher working on the period. This is some of the stuff we're likely to want for the programme. See. *(He points to a glossy pic of WAITE in '38, at the rostrum, at the TUC annual congress.)*

I asked her to look out the best pictures of you and
make them up into ... well, this. *(He hands the album
on to WAITE's knee.)* If it's of any interest.

WAITE: *(Turning pages)* Interest! I should say so. Yes!
Thank you. Ha, look at old Manny there ... He never
could resist a camera ...

MARIA: You can talk.

*(WAITE stares at a picture. We close on it. It's a
miners' picket in Manchester during the General Strike.
He's at its head, carrying the largest placard,
scrawny, freshfaced, scarf knotted at neck, cap on
head, thin trousers failing to reach his big boots.)*

WAITE: *(Very softly)* My God.

(WILLIAM looks over WAITE's shoulder at the picture.)

WILLIAM: *(As softly)* A man could die of memories like that.
*(He walks down the room towards the french windows.
MASSINGHAM stands.)*

MASSINGHAM: Well, I think I'll go up. You'll have plenty
to talk about, I imagine.

WAITE: *(Snapping the trance)* I thought you wanted to
discuss tomorrow ...

MASSINGHAM: *(Looking around)* Not er ... not if it's going
to get in the way of ...

WAITE: Nonsense.

(Looking to MARIA for support.)

Be a party piece. And it'll be something for William
to get his teeth into. *(Down room)* What do you say,
William?

WILLIAM: *(Turning)* What's that?

WAITE: We're going to talk about my interview. I said
you'd enjoy a bit of ... mental exercise.

(WILLIAM looks down at his glass, up the room again.)

WILLIAM: *(Finally)* Why not.

MARIA: *(To WAITE)* The doctor said an early night.

WAITE: I know what the doctor said and I'll still see him
out. Physician heal thyself, I said to *him*. That
shut him up. *(Generally)* Sit you down then. Let's
get cracking.

*(MASSINGHAM takes an armchair to the side of the large
fireplace. He's unhappy but senses no other option.
MARIA retains the chair opposite. WAITE closes the
album, rests it on his knee. WILLIAM refills his
glass, fills one for MARIA, carries it to her, perches,
remotely, on a small upright chair so that he can see
his father's face but so as to remain physically
peripheral to the action. He is taut, rather white,
growing grimmer.)*

(In good humour) What they call a talk-in, eh.

(To MASSINGHAM) Right. Off you go, young man.

MASSINGHAM: *(Smoothly)* I'd rather hoped you'd do the
talking, Mr Waite. *(Pause. Smile.)* It *is* your story.

WAITE: *(Teasing slightly)* Aren't you going to ask me
questions?

(MASSINGHAM remains blandly silent.)

Nay, if you don't ask me questions, I can't give you
answers.

MASSINGHAM: Couldn't we perhaps ... simply ... talk ...
generally. I'd prefer to keep your ... 'answers'
as ... fresh and spontaneous as possible ... for
tomorrow.

WAITE: I'm getting on, Mr Massingham. Maybe you haven't
noticed it, but I'm seventy-one. And old men do
tend to ramble a bit ... Still.

WILLIAM: *(Suddenly)* I'll ask you a question.

(Silence. WAITE looks at WILLIAM.)

40

WAITE: Is it ... germane?

WILLIAM: *I* think so.

(WAITE looks at MASSINGHAM, who smiles assent.)

WAITE: *(Putting empty pipe to mouth)* Ask your question.

WILLIAM: *(Very tense)* Given the power that you and your party have from time to time exercised in the last fifty years, and given the fact that your rhetoric is invariably radical in temper, how do you explain the extremely modest nature of the changes you have managed to effect?

WAITE: *(Blowing histrionically)* Is that the question, is that all of it?

(WILLIAM makes no answer.)

Well, let me begin by attacking the premise. Our achievements have been *far* from modest, and only a person blinded by dogma or utterly without acumen would fail to see it. There isn't a part of this society, top to bottom, that hasn't been profoundly affected by what we have done, in office and out. The record speaks for itself, but I'll speak to it if you'd like.

(WAITE looks in MASSINGHAM's direction.)

Do you want to hear it?

MASSINGHAM: *(Alert again)* Yes indeed.

WAITE: Where to begin? 1924? When we found ourselves a minority government at the mercy of a potential Tory-Liberal alliance and a hostile press, and still managed, in *months*, mind, not years, to honour our election promises over unemployment benefits, over the creation of new jobs in road and railway construction, over slum clearance and new housing subsidies, over education. 1929? Against a backcloth of shrinking world trade and a collapse in the world's financial

structures - and still at the mercy of Tory-Liberal
alliances - we were still able to raise and extend
the pensions of widows and the aged, we were still
able to make unemployment insurance more easily
available, we were still able to work for international
co-operation and disarmament. *(Pause)* I make no
apologies for the renegade Macdonald and the 1931
National Government. But you will remember that he
was rightly and promptly ejected by the party and
shunned by it thereafter. *(Pause)* The great Attlee
administrations of '45 to '51? There, surely, if
nowhere else. I say nothing of my own part. But
look at the record sometime, *objectively* - if I
might borrow an overworked word from you for a
moment. We said we must have full employment, and we
had it. For the first time in history, outside of
wars. We said we must control the commanding heights
of industry, and we took coal and the railways, road
transport, electricity, gas, iron and steel into
public ownership. We said we must have a say in the
way the country was financed, and we nationalised the
Bank of England. *(Pause)* And underpinning all of this,
we created a *caring* society, a community in which
people were entitled to a good education, to health
services, national assistance and pensions *as of
right*, not as charities doled out by this board or
that.
*(WAITE stops, wipes his forehead and neck with a
handkerchief, half-exhausted by his effort, suddenly
passionate, alive, no longer patronisingly remote.*
In six short years we created a social revolution.
And we did it with the consent of the people. And
nobody was shot or imprisoned or tortured or ... blown

42

up to effect it. *(Long pause.)* And we did it against a backcloth of financial crisis, world shortages of food, fuel and raw materials, a hostile civil service, a rabidly Tory press, and an international community determined to make the abandonment of our socialist policies the condition of making loan capital available. *(Pause. He's angry.)* Do I bring us up to date? Or do we just let the question quietly drop?

MARIA: *(To WILLIAM)* Leave it be.

WILLIAM: *(To WAITE)* Is that what *you* want?

WAITE: *(Angry)* Go ahead.

(WILLIAM gets up, carries his glass to the cabinet, speaking as he does so.)

WILLIAM: Let it drop.

WAITE: The hell we'll let it drop. Finish what you started.

WILLIAM: *(Turning sharply)* Look. You're old. And you're ill. And you're my father. There's no way I can win. I asked my question, you answered it.

WAITE: *(Deliberately)* Don't patronise me, sonny.

(WILLIAM turns back to the drinks, pours. Deliberates. Turns. MARIA and MASSINGHAM watch everything.)

WILLIAM: *(Finally, metallic)* All right. *(Pause)* Ramsay Macdonald boasted in 1923, 'We are going to make the land blossom like a rose and fill it with glorious aspirations'. When he came to power - the *first* Labour prime minister - a national daily argued that 'the party of revolution approach their hands to the helm of state with the design of destroying the very basis of civilised life'. *(To MASSINGHAM.)* I hope we get a chance to have a look at those ... dangerous men in your programme ... as they queued nervously in their bowlers and toppers and cutaway collars outside Buckingham Palace, to meet the Royal Person and prove the papers wrong. *(Back to WAITE.)* You make no case at all for them, beyond the tiniest ameliorations in lives impoverished and ghastly beyond belief, so there's little point in dwelling on them, save to point out that in the likes of Macdonald and Snowden the capitalist system found two of its ablest and most orthodox defenders in this century. *Labour* leaders. Leaders of the working class. *(Pause)* Like you.

(WILLIAM looks around the room, taking in the whole house, the whole life-style.)

Out of touch. Out of reach. Out of sympathy. Leaders.

WAITE: Nobody spent more time in his constituency than me and well you know it.

WILLIAM: Except you didn't *live* in it, did you?

WAITE: Of course I didn't. Because I worked in London.

WILLIAM: But you had a house in Manchester. Where we grew up. Only it wasn't in your constituency, was it? It was in Didsbury, four bedrooms, attics, cellars, gardens, playschools, parks ... Not the sort of house you'd find in Beswick now, was it? Because Beswick was single-class housing. *Working*-class.

WAITE: Would you have thanked me for a childhood spent in a dingy two-up two-down? Eh?

WILLIAM: *(Fiercely)* Yes! Yes! I would. Because then the rhetoric would have made sense. Because then the leaders and the led would have been part of the same *experience*, instead of just part of the same sentence.

WAITE: I never lost touch. Never. They'd've soon let me know if I had. Where it hurts most. In the

44

ballot box.

(WILLIAM walks about, regaining his balance, reaching for impersonality again.)

WILLIAM: No. It was the rhetoric you never lost. So that you can describe the Attlee legislation as a *social revolution* as though what happened during that time was what socialism is all about. A *real* social revolution would have committed you to the destruction of capitalism and the social order formed and maintained by it. A real social revolution would have effected major redistribution of *wealth*, in favour of the labouring masses. A real social revolution would have smashed the bourgeois state apparatus and begun the construction of a people's state. Courts, civil service departments, police, church, army, schools - nothing would have stayed the same. It wasn't a social revolution you achieved, it was a - as it turned out - minimal social adjustment. You drew a section of the working classes into the grammar schools, and allowed the public schools to continue training upper and middle class elites. You set up national insurance schemes and allowed private insurance to feed and grow fat on the great pond of fear remaining. You created a *national* health service and allowed the doctors to practise privately. You created municipal housing and left the building industry in the hands of the capitalists. You nationalised the ailing industries and services and allowed the strong to be run privately, for private profit. *(Pause)* You didn't create a new social order, you merely humanised the old one.

WAITE: Have you finished?

WILLIAM: I've barely started.

45

WAITE: It's all so easy, isn't it? You sit there behind your little desk in your little room in your little ivory tower and you read your Marx and your Trotsky and you get your slide rule out and do a couple of simple calculations and you have your blueprint. Revolution. Total change. Overnight. Bang. Especially bang. You have to have your bit of theatre as well, don't you? *(Pause)* Reality isn't like that. Reality is ... taking people with you. Arguing with people who disagree, passionately. It's fighting hostile influences, foreign investors, currency speculators. It's sweating on a good balance of trade surplus at the end of the month. Reality is priorities. You haven't the first idea.

WILLIAM: Maybe not. But I can recognise a shabby definition of reality when I hear it. Did it ever occur to you that Edward Heath might give exactly the same definition as the one you've just propounded? Is a socialist reality the same as a Tory one then?

WAITE: We live in the same world. It doesn't change because we shut our eyes and dream.

WILLIAM: It doesn't change *unless* we shut our eyes and dream. 'I take my desires for reality, because I believe in the reality of my desires.'

WAITE: Try doing a bit of leading some day. See where it gets you.

WILLIAM: *(Tough)* You didn't fail to deliver a social revolution because reality got in the road. You didn't deliver one because you didn't *want* one. You didn't *desire* one. In fact, you desired anything but.

WAITE: You'll learn.

WILLIAM: If there's one thing marks you all out - *(With great, deliberate emphasis.)* - labour ... leaders - it's

this desperate need to be accepted. You ... efface
yourselves until there's nothing there. You all want
to prove you can 'do the job as well as they can'.
As though that were the summit of socialist aspiration.
The need to be thought of as 'responsible' men.
Examine that ... seedy collection currently 'leading'
the party. Define their reality if you can. They
stand like adolescents at a dance, waiting to become
men. Churchill knew it, instinctively. 'Sheep in
sheep's clothing', he called you. 'An empty cab
arrived and Mr Attlee stepped out.' *(Pause)* It's a
sort of masochism you all have. It's not there in the
Tories, no fear. When a Tory minister calls at his
favourite whorehouse, he doesn't go to be beaten, he
goes to *beat*. He's *used* to it. You never will be.
(WAITE turning away towards MASSINGHAM, who sits,
tightlipped and intent.)

WAITE: I hope this is of some use to *you*. I'm damned if
it's of any to me. When a man gets down to quoting
Churchill at me, I know he's run out of an argument.
He talks about revolution but he forgets to talk
about politics.

WILLIAM: *(Fast)* Tell us about '26 then.

(Silence. Something dangerous is registered.)

MARIA: That's enough, William. It's been a long day.

WAITE: *(Ignoring her)* What would you like to hear?

WILLIAM: Wouldn't you have said '26 was a sort of
revolutionary moment?

WAITE: On the contrary, I'd've said it was the final and
crushing evidence that 'revolution', in your sense,
is not the English way of doing things.

WILLIAM: Is that what you believed at the time?

WAITE: I believed in the miners' cause at the time.

47

You'll recall I was a miner.

WILLIAM: You believed in all-out confrontation with the
owners and the state then.

WAITE: Yes I did, but I don't think I want ...

WILLIAM: You're a liar.

(Silence)

WAITE: Say that again.

WILLIAM: *(Deliberately)* You're a liar.

MARIA: *(Getting up)* All right, I've heard enough. *(To
WILLIAM)* I think you'd better leave before you do any
more damage.

WILLIAM: *(Lifting)* I'll leave when *he tells me to.*

MARIA: *(Going to push him out)* You'll leave *now.*

WILLIAM: *(Pulling violently away)* Leave me *alone.* I'm
not a bloody infant and neither is he.

MARIA: He's ill. Christ, do you want to kill him?

WAITE: Let him be, Maria.

MARIA: I won't. And you should grow up a little, a man
of your age and ... You're like children ... 'It's
me, it's me.' Jesus Christ. *(She pulls away.)* All
right, damn you both.

*(MARIA walks out of the room, angry, close to tears.
MASSINGHAM has stood up, wavers uncertainly. WAITE
and WILLIAM glare at each other.)*

MASSINGHAM: Would you ... rather I er ...

WAITE: *(Not looking at him)* No no. You should stay to
the end, Mr Massingham. After all, it's been created
in your honour.

*(MASSINGHAM sits. WAITE sits in MARIA's chair.
WILLIAM remains standing.)*

Let's have it then.

WILLIAM: *(Metallic again)* When I'm not devising
blueprints for revolution in that ivory tower of mine

the world otherwise knows as the University of
Manchester, I busy myself with a doctoral thesis on
the relationship between leaderships and grassroots
in working-class political organisations. Now that
may neither interest nor disturb you. What may come
as something of a surprise is the knowledge that over
the past six months I have had access to NUM files
- your union - for the year 1926. The year of the
General Strike. The year you made District
Association executive. *(Pause)* I've had a chance to
study your record during that crucial year. How you
spoke, how you voted. And I know now, absolutely,
what you've always been made of. *(Pause)* You opposed
the strike before it took place and you voted on no
less than six occasions after it for a return to work.
You didn't want it to take place, you didn't want it
to succeed. And when it was over, you acted as
vice-chairman on the committee that was set up with
the owners to agree on pay reductions and who would go
down the road. That's the *leadership* you offered.
And if that's what you call being *for* the miners, by
Christ I hope you never side with me.

WAITE: It's astonishing you had to go to the files.

WILLIAM: The votes were secret.

WAITE: But I could have told you. Of course the votes
were secret. But the majority always won. We each
registered what we believed in our hearts to be
right. And then we all pitched in, as democrats, to
implement the decisions of the majority. I did
nothing I'm ashamed of. Our position was hopeless,
in my view, both before, and after, the strike. The
strike proved nothing, achieved nothing, save more
redundancies.

WILLIAM: *(Hard)* The strike proved that men can find
extraordinary solidarity under the most appalling and
oppressive conditions. Given a leadership basing
itself on the reality of desire instead of the
irreality of rhetoric, who knows what it might not
have accomplished. *(Pause)* In any case, this part of
your life has hardly been an open book, has it?
(To MASSINGHAM) Did you know about it?

MASSINGHAM: *(Slowly)* No, I can't say I did ...

WILLIAM: And he's read your autobiography.

WAITE: A life's a long thing. A book can't hold it all.

WILLIAM: It will generally be found to hold what we
want it to.

WAITE: *(Standing slowly)* I stand on what I've done. I've
made mistakes, God knows. And usually I've paid for
them. But I believe I've given more than I've taken,
and helped more people than I've hurt. I agree with
Beatrice Webb about the General Strike and the
miners' strike that precipitated it. 'A proletarian
distemper', she called it, 'that had to run its
course'. Well, distemper's a kind of sickness, and
you can't build a new order on a sickness. *(Pause)*
As to desires and reality, the people have always
suffered from a poverty of desire, as my old friend
Ernie Bevin used to put it. We could have gone
faster, perhaps, but they wanted us to walk so that
they could see where we were going. *(Pause)* One day
you may find yourself doing something really serious,
like running a ministry, and then you'll see where
dreams get you. And now I'm going to bed. *(Looking
straight at WILLIAM.)* You make me tired. I'll see you
in the morning, Mr Massingham. Thank you for the
presents. Thank you both. *(He walks to the door. Turns*

Oh, one more betrayal you should know about, but
please keep it to yourself for the moment. I am to be
elevated to the peerage in the New Year. If you wish
to change your name by deed poll, I shall perfectly
understand. Goodnight.

(WAITE leaves.

WILLIAM stares after him, numb. MASSINGHAM crosses
to the drinks cabinet, pours himself a large scotch,
puts it back in two connected gulps, pours himself
another.)

MASSINGHAM: Excuse me.

(MASSINGHAM walks to the french windows.)

13. INT. CONSERVATORY. NIGHT

MASSINGHAM passes through to the conservatory, puts on a
single light, revealing floods and spots, in half rigged
state, for the morning. He plugs in at two different
plug boards, brings up the lights in turn, checking spot
focus on the two interview chairs, general spread
elsewhere.

After a moment, WILLIAM appears in the doorway, glass in
hand. He carries a small attache case.

WILLIAM: Lord Waite remembers. Your researchers should
    have found out about the pipe. It's a prop. He
    doesn't smoke it.

    (MASSINGHAM stops working for a moment to look at
    WILLIAM, then goes on. WILLIAM places the attache
    case on a cupboard, opens it, takes out a blue file.)

    I had some copies made of the miners' strike voting ...

MASSINGHAM: *(Looking at file)* What makes you think I'll
    use it?

WILLIAM: Won't you?

51

(MASSINGHAM takes the file, opens it, studies it a moment.)

MASSINGHAM: I don't know.

WILLIAM: *(Softly)* Yes you do. *(Pause)* You can't resist it

MASSINGHAM: I thought ... you were against me.

WILLIAM: Oh I am.

MASSINGHAM: *(File in air)* Then why this?

(WILLIAM closes the case, his back to MASSINGHAM.)

WILLIAM: I went to see a mate of mine in London this afternoon. Alwyn Bell. Works for your lot. Know him

MASSINGHAM: *(Guarded)* Not really. I see him at meetings from time to time.

WILLIAM: He knows you. *(Pause)* He says you're a crook.

MASSINGHAM: Really.

WILLIAM: He says you're well known in the features field for setting up fake projects in order to get other things done.

MASSINGHAM: Does he!

WILLIAM: He says if you're supposed to be doing a whitewash on a Labour politician you're almost certainly planning a hatchet job. *(Pause)* I trust Alwyn. *(Pause)* He's pretty certain there's no such series as 'Living History' on the stocks or projected.

MASSINGHAM: I told you, it's a working title. *(Silence)* So. If I'm firing, why not use some of your ammunition, is that it?

WILLIAM: Something like that. *(Pause)* Maybe I shouldn't even bother interfering. Leave you to each other. Maybe that way, *your* class loyalty and his ... objective treachery ... will stand out more clearly. *(Turning)* Attack him how you like.

MASSINGHAM: *(Quickly)* I can take it ... you won't be

speaking with him, can I?

WILLIAM: Yes. Do you think he'd listen? To me? In any
case, *he* needs you as much as you need him. After all,
you're both involved in ... mystifications, aren't
you?

MASSINGHAM: *(Angry now)* I've told you what I'm involved
in. I'm involved in making good programmes.

WILLIAM: *(Lifting)* Sure. And if that involves ridiculing
and sneering at a man who's spent the best part of
his life working and slaving, however benightedly,
to make things just a little bit better for people,
well, so be it, that's how the cookie crumbles when
the shit hits the fan etc. Eh? Yes? Because
nobody can take seriously, let alone imagine fit for
office, a man who likes HP Sauce, or Wincarnis, or
ducks in flight on the wall, can they? You can't
esteem a man who looks and talks like a *grocer*, can
you? How can you possibly listen to someone who's
been branded on the tongue! Oh God, if only the
eighteenth century hadn't gone wrong the way it did,
what a fine and ordered world we'd all be living in.

MASSINGHAM: Very satirical. Perhaps you should go in
for politics. You seem to have all the answers.
*(MASSINGHAM begins switching the lights off, picks up
the file, passes WILLIAM to go into the house.)*
I'd still sooner be me than you. Goodnight.
*(MASSINGHAM leaves, cool, unconcerned, already
working on tomorrow.*
*WILLIAM stands in the barely lit conservatory. Stares
at his father's chair. Approaches it. Runs his
fingers gently round the top rim. Steps backwards,
until he can sit facing it.)*

14. INT. BEDROOM. NIGHT

Waite's bedroom. WAITE lies awake, pillowless, staring
at the ceiling, in the dark room. His wife's voice cuts
the silence, metallic, like WILLIAM's.

ANN: *(V.O. - An elaborate sexual game)* Guttersnipe.
Prole. Rough ... diamond. Arriviste. *(Quickly)*
Stay down! *(Capping)* Collier!

> *(Knock at door. Another. MARIA in, in dressing*
> *gown. She stands in the doorway, listening.)*

MARIA: You awake?

WAITE: Aye. Come in.

> *(MARIA closes door to, crosses to the bed, flicks on*
> *a rather harsh wall-light, directed away from the*
> *bed but giving flareback from the smooth white wall.*
> *Sits carefully halfway down the bed.*

> *WAITE remains prostrate, fatigued but not sleepy.)*

MARIA: Are you going to be all right?

WAITE: Oh yes. I'm indestructible.

MARIA: I'll come at Christmas if you like.

WAITE: Be nice.

> *(Pause)*

MARIA: You mustn't let yourself get upset like that,
you know.

WAITE: He's like his mother. Stubborn. Even looks like
her.

MARIA: Get away. Spitting image of you.

> *(WAITE puts his hand out for MARIA's. Covers it.)*

WAITE: *You're* mine.

> *(Silence)*

MARIA: Dad.

WAITE: Mmm?

MARIA: Is there ... any chance of your not accepting the
life peerage?

WAITE: I've said yes. I can't go back on my word.
    (Pause) Do you think I should?

MARIA: You must do what you think's right. *(Pause)* You
    do ... despise it though, don't you? You don't
    believe it somehow ... honours you ...?

WAITE: Miner's lad to peer of the realm, or How I
    slipped from grace. *(Pause)* No no. Say, it suits my
    purpose and the party's. *(Pause)* You will ... accompany
    me, won't you?
    (Pause)

MARIA: *(Finally)* I don't think I can, Dad.
    (Silence)

WAITE: I see.

MARIA: It wouldn't be right, Dad. *(Pause)* I can't believe
    in a classless society and then suddenly one day -
    take part in their obscene pantomime. I couldn't
    keep faith with the poor kids I teach, if I did that.
    I spend most of my working life battling against
    privilege and ... hierarchy and inequalities of
    opportunity ...

WAITE: You make too much of it, lass. It's nobbut a
    little thing.

MARIA: Maybe. But sooner or later we've got to stop
    being ... picked off. Sucked in one by one, patted,
    flattered. We've got to stay with the class, Dad.
    We've got to say no. We go when the class goes. You
    can't lead an army in the uniform of the enemy.
    (Pause) I'm sorry.

WAITE: *(Smiling, patting her hand)* It's not been what
    you'd call my day, all in all, has it? Some days it's
    hardly worth getting out of bed. *(Pause)* Maybe it'll
    buck up tomorrow; let me sleep now.
    (MARIA gets up, switches out the light. Bends to kiss

WAITE on the forehead. Stands again.)

MARIA: Take care.

　　(WAITE nods, smiles.

　　MARIA reaches the door.)

WAITE: Mar. *(She turns, back-lit.)* Leave your mother's
　　address, will you? I'll drop her a line.

　　(MARIA smiles to herself at his blunt, uncomplicated
　　pragmatism. Leaves.)

15. INT. CONSERVATORY. DAY

Conservatory. Cameraman, assistant, lights, P.A., etc.
WAITE sits in his chair being dabbed by make-up.
The lights burst across his eyes. Voices blur around him.
MASSINGHAM talks quietly with the cameraman, gesturing a
lot; smiles reassuringly in WAITE's direction.
MARIA appears in the french windows, ready for off,
withdraws. MASSINGHAM sees her, detaches, follows her.
He carries his own file and WILLIAM's.

16. INT. LIVING ROOM. DAY

MARIA waits just inside the room.

MARIA: Goodbye, Mr Massingham.

MASSINGHAM: Goodbye, Mrs Bryant. I ... very much
　　enjoyed meeting you.

MARIA: *(Slowly)* Be careful with him, won't you?

MASSINGHAM: Yes of course.

MARIA: He's a good man.

　　(An uncomfortable silence between them.

　　MARIA turns away finally, leaves.

　　MASSINGHAM watches her, the files pulled in to his
　　chest. Returns to the conservatory.)

17. INT. CONSERVATORY. DAY

High shot of the conservatory.

MASSINGHAM takes his seat opposite WAITE, leans forward
to whisper some encouragement. Noises subsiding,
people taking up positions. They roll. Clapperboard.
C.U. WAITE. MASSINGHAM's voice over, muffled, distant.

MASSINGHAM: Lord Waite, I'd like to ask you about your
attitude to some of the really crucial moments in
the history of our society in this century. Take
1926, for example, and the General Strike. How would
you summarise your view of it now, half a century
later, and how would that view differ from your
feelings at the time? You were, of course, deeply
involved in the miners' strike of that year that
directly precipitated the General Strike.

(C.U. WAITE. All sound out. Light very white,
bright, washing out the shapes and textures of his
face.

His lips begin the answer.

Pull back very gradually, back and up until eventually
beyond the conservatory, mute, to reveal him in his
chair, alone, the room empty of equipment and people,
his baronet's robes draping his still form.

Fade out.)

ABSOLUTE BEGINNERS

Absolute Beginners was first broadcast by BBC TV on
19 April 1974 in the series 'Fall of Eagles'. The cast
was as follows:

VON PLEHVE	Bruce Purchase
NICHOLAS	Charles Kay
LENIN	Patrick Stewart
KRUPSKAYA	Lynn Farleigh
MARTOV	Edward Wilson
ZASULICH	Mary Wimbush
TROTSKY	Michael Kitchen
BAUMAN	Peter Weston
PLEKHANOV	Paul Eddington
ALEXANDROVA	Svandis Jons
LIEBER	David Freeman
TUPURIDZE	Julian Fox
KRASIKOV	Robert O'Mahoney
MARTINOV	Raymond Witch
NARRATOR	Michael Hordern
Costumes	Daphne Dare
Sound	Derek Miller-Timmins
Designer	Allan Anson
Producer	Stuart Burge
Director	Gareth Davies

CHARACTERS

LENIN

NADEZHDA KONSTANTINOVA KRUPSKAYA

JULIUS OSIPOVITCH MARTOV

VERA IVANOVNA ZASULICH

GEORGES VALENTINOV PLEKHANOV

LEON TROTSKY

N.E. BAUMAN

TUPURIDZE

ALEXANDROVA

LIEBER

MARTINOV

NICHOLAS II

VON PLEHVE

LANDLADY, Holford Square

KRASIKOV

Non-speaking

ALEXANDER POTRESOV

PAVEL BORISOVITCH AXELROD

GUARD

SHOTMAN

LENGNIK

KRZIZHANOVSKI

AKIMOV

'CENTRE' DELEGATES TO CONGRESS

OTHER 'HARD' DELEGATES

'RIGHT' DELEGATES

PLEKHANOV'S TEENAGE DAUGHTERS (12, 14)

SETS: State Room, Tsarskoe Selo. Holford Square:
Study/Bedroom; Kitchen/Living Room. Commune,
Sidmouth Street (one room). Plekhanov's Study.
Warehouse Office, Brussels. Lecture Theatre, London.
Caucus Room.

TELECINE: Von Plehve's armoured carriage, Tsarskoe Selo.
Estates, Tsarskoe Selo. British Museum, Forecourt etc.
Train to Geneva. Highgate Cemetery.

1. INT. TSARSKOE SELO STATE ROOM. DAY

Von Plehve, large, massy, bearded, at the huge window,
looking down at the formal lawns and curved drive at the
front of the house. His coach stands there, four armed
police at ease around it.

TELECINE 1:

Ext. Driveway. Day

The POLICEMEN share a cigarette. We examine the coach
through the movement. It is heavily armoured, with thick
zinc plating at the windows and double locks at the door.

2. INT. STATE ROOM. DAY

State Room. VON PLEHVE turns as the door is opened at
the far end of the long room and NICHOLAS enters.
VON PLEHVE bows low. NICHOLAS advances briskly into the
room, untrapping his shirt collar as he goes.

NICHOLAS: Von Plehve.

PLEHVE: Your Majesty.

> *(NICHOLAS sits at the head of the long table, where*
> *PLEHVE has laid his 'report': files, dossiers,*
> *photographs.)*

NICHOLAS: *(Reading, studying)* I've been ... shooting ...
> *(Shy smile at PLEHVE; polite smile back.)*
> Mmm. Is this everything?

PLEHVE: If Your Majesty would care to compare it with
last year's report, I think he will find an agreeable
improvement in the country's security.

63

(NICHOLAS already beginning to use files as cover.)

NICHOLAS: I think you should know, Plehve, that only yesterday I received a security report from Colonel Zubatov. Admittedly his provenance is limited to labour unrest ... but there is little doubt in his mind that there has been a disagreeable deterioration in security. *(Pause)* Mmm?

PLEHVE: With respect, Majesty, I do what I can. *(Pause)* It is precisely Zubatov's police union policies that undermine my own efforts to promote discipline and the rule of law.

(NICHOLAS studying pictures again.)

NICHOLAS: *He*, of course, lays exactly the same charge against *you*.

(Looking at PLEHVE seriously, like a young boy, but with irony too.)

I would like some guidance.

PLEHVE: Majesty, the state has no business organising workers to present economic demands to employers. There are plenty of ... revolutionists around to do that, God knows. The state's job is containment. We put out fires. And we eliminate fire raisers. The market and tradition ... will take care of the rest.

(NICHOLAS enjoying his game: somehow incapable of proper seriousness: yet not joking.)

NICHOLAS: But it *was* Zubatov who organised 50,000 workers or more in a demonstration of loyalty to the throne in Moscow last month, wasn't it?

PLEHVE: *(Hard)* Majesty, in Zlatoust, last week, one of those same ... unions stormed the offices of the Urals Mining Federation ...

NICHOLAS: *(Quickly)* Why do I not know about this?

PLEHVE: It's in the report. *(Pause)* It is hardly a

64

singular event, Majesty. *(Pause)* I have the situation under control.

NICHOLAS: I'm relieved to hear it. *(Pause)* Jews, was it?

PLEHVE: Jews, anarchists, revolutionists ... fortunately they're all the same size in a gun-sight. *(Pause)* Sixty-nine rioters killed; a hundred and forty-three wounded; over two hundred arrests. Two dozen already hanged. *(Pause)* It's all there.

(PLEHVE points to large file.

NICHOLAS opens the file rather woodenly, psychologically too weak by far for a close scrutiny.)

(With an advantage) I ordered a grenadier regiment up from Orenburg to burn a few houses and restore order.

(NICHOLAS nods several times.)

And ... I ... took the liberty of drafting a message of congratulations to the officers commanding.

(PLEHVE plucks it from a file, hands it to Nicholas.)

It would be a considerable boost to morale if you would consent to sign it, Majesty.

(NICHOLAS putting it down.)

NICHOLAS: Yes, of course.

PLEHVE: *(Relentless)* We will win the war if we have the will to, Majesty. But ... they must be made to understand that we are serious. And if we are to be serious we must be coherent, we must be ruthless, and above all we must be intelligent. That is the message you will find in every page of my report, Majesty.

(NICHOLAS bites his lip, breathes deeply, gets up, turns to the window. Silence.)

NICHOLAS: I shot seven crows this morning. *(Pause)* Are they all ... my enemies?

PLEHVE: Potentially. As they are all your loyal and devoted friends and subjects. The people ... are simply the stakes, Your Majesty.

NICHOLAS: And whom do we ... play for them?

PLEHVE: They're all there.

(PLEHVE waves an experienced hand across the files
of pictures.)

Socialist-Revolutionaries. Anarchists. Liberals.
Social-Democrats ...

(NICHOLAS at table again, studying pictures.)

NICHOLAS: Jew. Jew. Jew. Aren't there *any* Russians?

PLEHVE: One or two, Your Majesty.

(PLEHVE begins spreading mug shots on the table.)
NICHOLAS crosses reluctantly to look at them.)

NICHOLAS: Look at them.

(We see their distasteful faces: PLEKHANOV, AXELROD,
ZASULICH, POTRESOV, STRUVE, BAUMAN, MARTOV, TROTSKY ...
KRUPSKAYA ... LENIN.)

(V.O.) Who are these?

PLEHVE: *(V.O.)* Social democrats. Dreamers mostly.
Marxists, they call themselves. *(PLEKHANOV)*
Plekhanov, Geneva. The leading figure.

NICHOLAS: *(We reach MARTOV)* This one. Jew, yes?

PLEHVE: Martov. Born ... Tsederbaum.

NICHOLAS: *(To LENIN)* And this?

(PLEHVE turns picture over for legend.)

PLEHVE: Ulyanov. Agitator. Fourteen months in the
Marinka awaiting trial. Sentenced to three years
exile '97. Menusinsk. Last report has him in ...
Munich. Married to this one here. *(KRUPSKAYA. V.O.*
drily.) Maybe she'll give him some babies ... make
him settle down, in Germany.

(Back to LENIN picture.
Mix to C.U. LENIN, PLEHVE's voice continues.)

(V.O.) Of course my political police abroad are

monitoring their every movement.

3. INT. HOLFORD SQUARE. DAY

The LENINS' two-room flat. The bedroom-study.

LENIN, trousers, boots, doing his fifty press-ups. He's at
forty; says it under his breath. Half-opened cases
litter the room.

Track into next room: forty-four, forty-five.

KRUPSKAYA prepares a frugal breakfast, turns to watch him
through the open adjoining door.

Knocking at door. LENIN stops, at full stretch. They
look at each other. LENIN hits fifty, stands, dons vest,
shirt, waistcoat, jacket, all neatly hung for him.

KRUPSKAYA opens door.

LANDLADY: Mrs ... *(She looks at her book.)* Richter?

    (KRUPSKAYA makes no answer, beyond a vague, staying
    frown.)

    I'm ... your landlady. Pleat, Mrs Pleat.
    (She's advancing into the room.) I believe my husband
    let you in last evening ... *(She's clocking everything,*
    talking to cover it.) I was at my sister's, she's had
    another of her turns, it's this weather I'm afraid,
    you'll find it the very devil to get used to, I
    shouldn't wonder. From ... Germany, isn't it?
    (LENIN in from the bedroom, dressed, a perfect
    bourgeois.)
    And you'll be Dr Richter, I presume.
    (LENIN looks at KRUPSKAYA.)
    I'm your landlady, Mrs Pleat. Well ... welcome to
    London. I hope your stay will prove a happy one.

KRUPSKAYA: Thank you. I'm sure it shall.

LANDLADY: *(Near door again)* Ah. While I remember. There is the matter of ... erm ... marriage lines.

KRUPSKAYA: I'm sorry ...?

LANDLADY: Please don't imagine I am in any way attempting
to pry ... It is simply that the authorities do demand
that I satisfy myself, as your legal landlady, as it
were, that you are ... well ... married. A ...
marriage certificate would ... *(Fade into silence.)*

KRUPSKAYA: *(To LENIN)* Isn't that in the large trunk?
(LENIN nods. MRS PLEAT smiles expectantly.)
Yes, I thought so. I'm afraid the large trunk is
travelling separately and won't be here for some
little while. *(Pause, studying effect.)* There is a *ring*
... if you'd care to see it ...
(KRUPSKAYA crosses to a box on the mantelpiece.
Produces their crude copper ring. MRS PLEAT takes it,
relieved.)

MRS PLEAT: Ah. How ... er ... unusual. Yes, that's
er ... Not that *I* doubted for one ... Well, thank
you.
(MRS PLEAT turns to LENIN, who remains silent, aloof.)
Nice to make your acquaintance, doctor ...
(MRS PLEAT's gone.
KRUPSKAYA pulls a cool, amused face at LENIN. He's
very serious. Approaches her.)

LENIN: I didn't know ... you still had it.

KRUPSKAYA: *(Simply)* I thought it might be useful
sometime.
(KRUPSKAYA smiles very seriously. LENIN touches the
hair on her forehead with the backs of his fingers.)
(Still held) Come. You'll be late for the printer.
And you have Martov and Zasulich to contact.
(LENIN nods. Releases KRUPSKAYA from his gaze.)
(Looking down, almost shy) I made breakfast.

68

TELECINE 2:

Ext. British Museum. Day

*LENIN stands on pavement outside British Museum, the
building clearly visible behind him through the railings.
He carries a roll of galleys under his left arm; stares
sombrely at the entrance of the pub across the way.
MARTOV emerges, studying a piece of paper in his hand,
looks around until he sees LENIN, breaks into smile,
hurries, despite the limp, across the road. He's thin,
smallish, bearded, untidy; papers and pamphlets bulge
from his person.*

MARTOV: Volodya!

    (Closing in, hugging him passionately.)

    Volodya, Volodya.

    (They kiss. A love kiss of sorts.)

    It's good to have you with us, comrade. *(Steps back.)*

    Let me look ... We expected you Wednesday.

LENIN: *(Smiling gently)* That's what Zasulich said.

MARTOV: Ah.

LENIN: She told me I'd find you ...

    (He waves towards the pub.)

MARTOV: *(Serious)* You know me. I need an argument. I
    need ... dialectic.

LENIN: *(Softly)* Today *is* Wednesday, Julius.

    *(MARTOV frowns, looks about him eccentrically, as
    though for confirmation, gropes at his pockets,
    smiles owlishly.)*

MARTOV: You know, I believe you're right, comrade. Shall
    we drink to that? Your note *(Paper in his hand.)*
    forced me to defer my destruction of the anarchists'
    position. It's a great place for anarchists is
    London, Volodya ...

LENIN: *(Indicating British Museum)* Let's talk, eh?

MARTOV: *(Serious)*   Of course.

> *(We watch them walk, arm in arm, into the British Museum forecourt.)*

Ext. Portico

LENIN and MARTOV stand beneath the Portico.
MARTOV has his glasses on the end of nose, totally engrossed in their exchange. He's studying a page of LENIN's Iskra *galleys.*
Looks up at LENIN, perhaps for an answer.
LENIN: A year. *(Pause)* Not less.

> *(MARTOV thinks.)*

MARTOV: Can we do it in a year?

LENIN: Yes. With work.

MARTOV: What does Plekhanov think?

LENIN: Does it matter? Plekhanov couldn't organise a
   coach to the theatre, and God knows he's had enough
   practice. In any case, he's a *theoretician*.
   Organisation isn't ... abstract enough for Georges.

MARTOV: But has he approved the broad strategy?

LENIN: Plekhanov and Axelrod have agreed to leave it to
   my judgement. That's to say, they support my view
   that we should not undertake a full Party Congress
   until our own tendency has been strengthened at the
   expense of all other tendencies. When the *Iskra*-men
   have a strong position within the party on the ground,
   then we can convene a congress that will recognise
   us as the leading element. And that won't happen until
   Iskra (He indicates the galleys.) has won the minds of
   the party workers.

MARTOV: *(Grinning suddenly)*   Oh how we've *missed you*,
   comrade.

4.   INT.   'COMMUNE' MAIN ROOM.   DAY

Table in centre.   LENIN, MARTOV, KRUPSKAYA, ZASULICH.
On the table, the Iskra *galleys and KRUPSKAYA's pinned*
map of Russia.
ZASULICH: 50, tall, handsome still but seeding fast, in
dressing gown, cigarette in mouth, cuts up bacon into
tiny pieces with a pair of nail scissors throughout
LENIN's speech.
On a board before her, chopped carrots, potatoes, onions,
etc.
LENIN bringing speech to a close.

LENIN: What we have now is a fragile chain of agents and
contacts spread thin across Russia; in a year, we
must have built the embryo of a party, each cell
working implicitly from the nucleus, the centre, the
source of power. At the moment, *they* are strong.
It's we who are weak. We're ... emigrés.
Dilettante, intellectual. Unreliable. We must
change that. We must begin with ourselves, if we
are to create an organisation of professional
revolutionaries whose duty is to devote not only
their free evenings but their whole life to working
for the Revolution. And when we have such an
organisation we will begin to shape the party in its
image.

(A small silence develops.)

ZASULICH: What does Georges say?

LENIN: *(Looking at MARTOV)* He agrees. *(Pause)* I don't
argue there isn't important work to be done *with* the
liberals, as with other elements. I simply say that
we must distinguish ourselves *organisationally* from
them, based on our profound theoretical differences.

MARTOV: Ilyich is right. We have to establish an

entirely new relationship between centre and
periphery. Just how to achieve the delicate balance
to strengthen central direction without endangering
local responsibility and initiative, is another
matter.

LENIN: Do you have ... suggestions?

MARTOV: One or two. I think I'd probably want a wider
membership than you appear to envisage. And I'd want
more power in the hands of the local committees.
But they're very minor. As I say, on the whole I
agree with your perspective.

LENIN: Vera Ivanovna?

ZASULICH: Well, if Georges says so, I don't suppose I'll
object. It seems a pity about the peasants.

LENIN: What does?

ZASULICH: They have revolutionary potential too. They
need ... organising too.

LENIN: They won't make the revolution. The question of
the peasant arises after the revolution, when they
are forced to bow to the dictatorship of the
proletariat. We'll see then how revolutionary they
are.

ZASULICH: It seems a bit late leaving it till then,
comrade. What do you propose to do about it *then*,
may I ask? Shoot them all? There are millions of
them.

LENIN: I'll discuss that at length with you some other
time, comrade Zasulich. At the moment, I'd prefer
we stayed with the agenda.
*(ZASULICH lights a cigarette, angry at the snub.
MARTOV catches LENIN's eye, tells him to go easy.)*
That becomes the policy then.
(LENIN stands up, preparing to go.)

We're building an army, comrades. And an army must
have its general staff. *(He spreads a hand.)* Us,
comrades. We have a newspaper. We have an
organisation. Now we must find the will. Then we
will be fit to lead.
(LENIN leaves, KRUPSKAYA follows, kissing ZASULICH
and muttering good night.
ZASULICH sweeping up food in a bowl, walking towards
kitchen.
To MARTOV, over shoulder.)

ZASULICH: Comrade Robespierre: you're too *soft* with him,
Julius.
(MARTOV looks as though he might follow LENIN, stops
himself, rubs his nose, thinking.)

5. INT. LENIN'S BEDROOM. NIGHT

Beds as before. Light from the street.
LENIN's watch ticks on the bed cupboard. After 2 a.m.
KRUPSKAYA and LENIN lie on their backs, awake.
LENIN withdrawn, brooding.

KRUPSKAYA: Do you want me?

LENIN: No.

KRUPSKAYA: Do you want to talk?

LENIN: *(Finally)* Perhaps we're the wrong people.

KRUPSKAYA: No.
(LENIN turns to look at KRUPSKAYA, plays with the hair
on her forehead a moment.)

LENIN: They're turning into fossils, Nadya. *(Long, tough*
pause.) Emigrés.

6. INT. LENIN'S KITCHEN/LIVING ROOM. NIGHT

KRUPSKAYA, expressionless, beginning delicate job of heating a coded letter. On the wall behind her, the map, red pins slightly more numerous. We see the cyrillic begin to take shape between the lines of the visible letter. A stew bubbles on the stove which, from time to time, she stirs, but functionally, undomestically. ZASULICH sits at the table drinking a glass of tea and smoking.

ZASULICH: Will we ever go back, Nadya, do you think ...?

> *(KRUPSKAYA, not turning, absorbed in the letter.)*

KRUPSKAYA: Oh yes.

ZASULICH: I want to believe that. Here we become ... nothing. Living or dying ...

7. INT. LENIN'S BEDROOM/STUDY. NIGHT

LENIN writes at his desk, whispers what he writes, but only half intelligibly.

LENIN: *(Whisper, finding the words)* ... not time to think about ... toy forms of democracy ... an organisation of real revolutionaries will stop at nothing ... rid itself of an undesirable member ...

8. INT. KITCHEN. NIGHT

ZASULICH: Nobody'll miss me, depend on it. When I go you'll say, dear me, we're drinking one glass of tea less ... and that'll be me. Aiii.

KRUPSKAYA: *(Turning, serious)* The revolution will not forget Zasulich, Vera Ivanovna. *(Pause)* The revolution will honour her.

9. INT. BEDROOM. DAWN

KRUPSKAYA sleeps in the bed. LENIN sits forward, head on one hand, pale, awake, the same touch, hunched position, reading what he has written. He flexes his writing hand, turns a final page or two. Three huge, spaced bangs on the front door knocker below. LENIN sits up, looks at the bed.

KRUPSKAYA sits, wide awake.

KRUPSKAYA: Was it there?

   (LENIN nods.)

   Then it's us.

LENIN: *(Checking watch)* At ten to five?

   (KRUPSKAYA sweeps into dressing gown and slippers, leaves quickly.)

10. INT. FRONT DOOR/HALL. DAY

KRUPSKAYA at door. She sees outline figure through glass. Opens door as hand goes up to knocker.

KRUPSKAYA: Yes?

   (A young man, TROTSKY, 23, tall, good looking, a bit of a dandy, in the doorway, a running taxi beyond.)

TROTSKY: Mrs ... Richter?

KRUPSKAYA: Who wants to know?

TROTSKY: *(Importantly)* Trotsky.

   (He waits. No response.)

   Bronstein.

   (Still no response.)

   Erm ... The Pen.

   (KRUPSKAYA smiles slowly, opens the door to admit him.)

KRUPSKAYA: Welcome, comrade. I'm ... M. Never forget the forms, comrade. We heard you were on your way.

> *(She looks at her watch.)* But I won't pretend we
> were ... expecting you exactly. Come.
>
> *(KRUPSKAYA moves for the stairs.)*

TROTSKY: Comrade.

> *(KRUPSKAYA turns. TROTSKY takes out a bank note.)*
> Would you be so good as to pay the cabbie for me. He
> seems to be having difficulty making himself understood
> *(KRUPSKAYA smiles, takes the money.)*

KRUPSKAYA: First on the right, on the next floor.

> *(TROTSKY smiles, heads for the stairs.)*

11.   INT.   KITCHEN/LIVING ROOM.   DAY

The door is open.   TROTSKY knocks, waits, enters.
LENIN appears in the adjoining doorway.

TROTSKY: Comrade Lenin?

> *(Pause.*
>
> *LENIN looks TROTSKY over, gives nothing.)*
> Trotsky. The Pen. Your wife let me in ... She's
> paying the taxi.

LENIN: Trotsky? I thought you were Bronstein.

TROTSKY: Bronstein I got tired of.

> *(Pause.*
>
> *Still little give there.)*
> Trotsky I borrowed from a gaoler ... just before I
> escaped. *(Pause)* Do you think it suits?
> *(LENIN still scrutinising, ignores the question and
> its irony.)*

LENIN: Do you have a letter? Something?

TROTSKY: *(Finally, to inside pocket)* Of course.

> *(TROTSKY hands the letter over.*
>
> *LENIN breaks open, reads. He looks over at TROTSKY
> once. Folds it neatly, returns letter to envelope.)*

LENIN: Welcome to London, comrade.

(They break at last, take each other in arms, hug.)

TROTSKY: It's an honour to be here, Comrade Lenin. I'm in your hands. Tell me what I can do.

LENIN: *(Watch)* Are you tired?

TROTSKY: No. Why do you ask?

(LENIN, closing watch. Small smile.)

LENIN: It doesn't matter. *(Pause)* Come. *(Beckoning into study.)* Sit down then. First of all you can tell me what you know. People, organisation, trends - everything ... A centre cannot hold without intelligence ...

(KRUPSKAYA appears in the adjoining doorway.
LENIN breaks off.)

KRUPSKAYA: Tea?

LENIN: Coffee. You've met our new comrade.

KRUPSKAYA: 'The young eagle' wasn't it Zaphorhets called him.

TROTSKY: It's something to do with the way I hold my nose, I think.

(KRUPSKAYA laughs.)

KRUPSKAYA: *(Leaving)* We need all the eagles we can get.

(TROTSKY returns his attention to LENIN.)

LENIN: Tell me.

TROTSKY: Do you mind if I remove my shoes?

LENIN: *(Puzzled)* Not at all. Please.

TROTSKY: *(Beginning to slip them off)* Ahh. *They* belonged to Trotsky too. You'd think the least they could do is provide warders with sensible feet.

(TROTSKY grins, wiggling his toes. LENIN smiles, sits back, studies him, liking the confidence, the style.
Mid-evening. Dark again outside. TROTSKY's shoes where they were. LENIN sits in his desk chair, facing

TROTSKY.

TROTSKY reads from his recent pamphlet Optimism and
Pessimism. *KRUPSKAYA at the kitchen table, coding a
stack of LENIN letters, mounds of* Iskra *around her,
awaiting despatch.*

*LENIN's room has grown cluttered through the day with
cups, plates, books, papers. The two men have talked
non-stop.)*

TROTSKY: *(Reading)* 'If I were one of the celestial bodies,
I would look with complete detachment upon this
miserable ball of dirt and dust ... I would shine
upon the good and the evil alike ... But I am a *man*.
World history ...

*(Cut to KRUPSKAYA, coding in kitchen. TROTSKY's voice
in background.)*

... which to you, dispassionate gobbler of science, to
you, book-keeper of eternity, seems only a negligible
moment in the balance of time, is to me everything!
As long as I breathe, I shall fight for the future,
that radiant future in which man, strong and
beautiful, will become the master of the drifting
stream of his history, and will direct it towards
the boundless horizon of beauty, joy and happiness.
It seems as if the new century, this gigantic
newcomer, were bent at the very moment of its
appearance, on driving the optimist into total
pessimism and civil nirvana ...'

LENIN: *(Very slow, broken up. Low, V.O.)* Are you doing
anything at all about *organisation* ... Once again I
earnestly beseech and demand that you write us more
often and in greater detail. In particular - do it
at once, without fail, the very same day you
receive this letter. Let us know you have received it,

even if only a couple of lines ...

(Cut to TROTSKY.)

TROTSKY: 'Surrender, you pathetic dreamer. Here I am, your long-awaited twentieth century, your future.'

'No', replies the unbowed optimist; 'You are only the present.'

(Silence. TROTSKY closes the pamphlet, looks almost shyly at LENIN. LENIN stares back.)

LENIN: Have you shown it to Plekhanov?

TROTSKY: No. He's seen other things of mine.

LENIN: And?

TROTSKY: He thinks my style is ... florid and rhetorical. *(Pause)* What do you think?

LENIN: He's right. *(TROTSKY frowns suddenly.)* But Georges has always put style first. He's a great ... European. *(Smiling chillily.)* He once said, not long ago even, that I had ... no style at all ... in the French sense, of course. *(TROTSKY grins suddenly.)* It's not the style that bothers me. I think it's too ... soft.

TROTSKY: I don't understand ...

LENIN: All right. How do we achieve that 'future' you talk of?

TROTSKY: By struggle. How else?

LENIN: But against whom?

TROTSKY: The state. And the classes whose interest it protects.

(Pause)

LENIN: The duty of a revolutionary is to fight those forces and personalities ... that obstruct and impede the socialist revolution ...

TROTSKY: That's what I said ...

LENIN: No. It isn't what you said and you must see the

difference. The 'future' is less than six months
away. We make the future every new theory we evolve,
every organisational change we set in progress.
(Pause) There will *be* no *revolution - Millions* will
not be mobilised to overthrow the Tsarist state
- unless *we* make it possible. We are Marxists: we
understand, as liberals and anarchists cannot, the
nature of power, of the state and so on. But it is
not enough to *know* the world; we must learn how to
change it. And that means, first and foremost,
building an organisation - a party - to develop the
theory and lead the revolutionary struggle. *(Pause)*
Do you see what I'm saying ...? *(Deliberately)*
Objectively, the enemy can be your best friend, your
lover, your party colleague, the chairman of your
local committee, the editor of your party journal ...
The enemy is he who impedes the course of the
revolution. *(Pause)* The real battle for now is not
with the Tsar, Comrade Trotsky; it's with ourselves.
(LENIN breaks off.

KRUPSKAYA appears in the doorway.)
KRUPSKAYA: If Comrade Trotsky doesn't leave soon he'll
miss Vera Ivanovna's mutton stew.
LENIN: All right.
(KRUPSKAYA returns to the kitchen.)
Think about it. I want you to stay for a while. Work
with *Iskra*. Find yourself. *(Pause)* A word of warning.
Don't become ... an emigré. These capital cities ...
fat, bourgeois ... they suck you in, if you let them.
Live only for the revolution in Russia. Do you
understand me?
TROTSKY: Yes. I saw a fair bit of it in Paris on my way
here.

LENIN: You'll see it here too.

>   *(Another discussion already in mind ...)*

>   Tell me about Paris ...

TROTSKY: *(Squeezing shoes on painfully)* Paris ... is
like Odessa. Only Odessa is better. *(Standing up.)*
I'm sorry, comrade. I mustn't miss my mutton stew.
*(They shake hands. TROTSKY passes into kitchen area,
where KRUPSKAYA gives him an address and a hand
sketch of the block. He kisses her forehead gently,
leaves. KRUPSKAYA closes the door after him. Comes
back into the study/bedroom. LENIN has already begun
work at his desk. She stands behind him. Gently
massages his neck and shoulder muscles. LENIN releases
his pen, sinks a little into the massage.)*

KRUPSKAYA: Was there anything for me?

>   *(LENIN weary; the news is old; he's known it for
>   years now.)*

LENIN: The Jewish Workers' Alliance are determined to
fight for control over their own affairs within the
party. *(Pause)* The 'Southern Worker' group argue that
we 'underestimate the role of the peasant', deplore
our sharp attacks on the liberals, and ... seek to
control their own affairs within the party. The
'Economists' group continue to argue in favour of
strictly industrial action and agitation, with the
problem of revolution to be left until the
bourgeoisie have captured power in Russia ... and seek
to control their own affairs within the party. *(Pause)*
It's not a party they want, it's a gentleman's club.

KRUPSKAYA: Come to bed now.

LENIN: I have less than a fortnight to finish my draft
programme for the board meeting ...

KRUPSKAYA: You'll work better tomorrow when you've slept.

Come. I'll sing.

(They're in bed, LENIN's head in KRUPSKAYA's arms.
She sings a Russian song, low, husky. She finishes;
strokes his head gently.)

Do you think we'll ever go home?

LENIN: Yes.

KRUPSKAYA: When?

LENIN: When the revolution needs us.

KRUPSKAYA: Shall I sing 'Katya'?

LENIN: No. No more music. It's too ... moving. *(Pause)*
It softens.

(Same scene. KRUPSKAYA sleeps. A clock booms three
a.m. LENIN sits at his desk, writing, muttering,
scratching out.)

12. INT. COMMUNE MAIN ROOM. DAY

MARTOV pours wine round the table. LENIN in the chair;
ZASULICH; KRUPSKAYA (taking notes); TROTSKY (though not
an Iskra board member) at end opposite chair. LENIN has
no glass. The others receive refills. Room rather cool.
ZASULICH fuming silently at LENIN. LENIN steely.

MARTOV:*(Talking gently)* Now let's keep calm. We're
comrades. These are honest differences and it's
right we should talk them out. But I see no need for
personalities and name-calling. Surely we're beyond
that sort of thing. I beg you, comrades ...
(MARTOV finishes his conciliatory libation, returns
to his chair, makes a worried face at LENIN.)

LENIN: *(Deliberately)* Do you have more criticism of my
programme, Vera Ivanovna?

(ZASULICH goes to asnwer but is headed off by MARTOV.)

MARTOV: *(Quiet, firm)* I think Vera Ivanovna has made her

point, Ilyich. It's quite simple. She prefers
Plekhanov's draft to yours. As do Axelrod and Georges
himself. You, Potresov and I prefer yours. If you
press for a vote, you give comrade Plekhanov, as
chairman of the *Iskra* Board, the opportunity of
casting the deciding vote in his own favour.
(MARTOV waits a moment, drinks some wine.)
May I make a suggestion?

LENIN: Please do.

MARTOV: Give me the two drafts. I'll see if I can't get
something out of them to please everybody.
(LENIN considers this.)

LENIN: What do you think, Comrade Trotsky?
(Some frowns. TROTSKY surprised.)
As a comrade, I mean.

TROTSKY: I think it's probably possible to safeguard
your salient points within Plekhanov's text.
Personally, I think Plekhanov's draft is better suited
for a textbook of economics than a party programme.

ZASULICH: Look, young man, Georges Plekhanov was running
a revolutionary movement when your father and mother
were still holding hands in the front parlour!

TROTSKY: *(Softly)* Yes, I know. He told me.

LENIN: All right. I accept what you say, Julius. But
it's important to preserve the notion of an all-out
attack on both absolutism *and* capitalism; and it
must be clearly understood, through the programme we
eventually agree, that the 'dictatorship of the
proletariat' means *just that* ... It does *not* mean
the dictatorship of the proletariat in conjunction with
the peasants. With those conditions, I concede the
need to prepare a new programme based on both drafts.
(Long pause. MARTOV winks at ZASULICH.)

It looks like July, comrades. We are strong and as
ready as we'll ever be. If Julius's Organising
Committee does its work properly, there should be no
difficulty in winning a majority for our programme
and party rules. What's the latest on Congress
venue, Julius?

MARTOV: Plekhanov and Alexrod favour Brussels. *(Pause)*
The Organising Committee is still undecided.

LENIN: *(Nodding)* Questions? Good.

(LENIN starts to get up.)

MARTOV: Would you mind staying a little longer, Ilyich?

*(LENIN looks surprised. MARTOV looks at ZASULICH and
TROTSKY before going on. LENIN sits down, frowning.
MARTOV takes an opened envelope from his pocket,
removes the letter, opens it up.)*

A ... comrade has asked if he might address the board?
He's waiting upstairs now.

LENIN: Upstairs? *(Pause. To KRUPSKAYA.)* Why is it not in
the agenda?

(KRUPSKAYA is bewildered.)

MARTOV: Comrade Miliutin arrived only this afternoon.
From Orlov. I raise the matter only now because I
didn't want the main body of the meeting to be
disrupted.

LENIN: *(Already sensing something)* I see. What does
Comrade ... Miliutin want?

MARTOV: I think he should be allowed to tell us that
himself.

LENIN: *(Finally unbudging)* Nevertheless ...

(Silence. MARTOV undecided. LENIN waits.)

MARTOV: Comrade Miliutin has laid grave charges against
one of our agents.

LENIN: *(Fast)* Who?

84

MARTOV: N.E. Bauman.

LENIN: What charges?

MARTOV: Bauman got Miliutin's wife with child during his
exile in Orlov. After his escape, he began to ...
slander her, labelled her 'the whore of Orlov', even
used our own underground networks to ... revile her.
It wasn't long, naturally, before party workers in
Orlov picked up the stories. *(Pause)* To ... *(Long
pause)* ... 'defend her honour', as she put it, she ...
hanged herself. *(Holds up letter.)* This is her
suicide note. It's addressed to the party. Vera
Ivanovna has already seen it.
*(MARTOV pushes the note towards LENIN, who picks it
up, reads it impassively, pushes it back down the
table.)*

LENIN: *(Mildly)* So.

(Not a question: a sort of new paragraph.)

MARTOV: Will you see him?

LENIN: No.

*(Silence. A slow stunned reaction. ZASULICH bangs
her huge fist into the table, spilling wine all over
it in her anger.)*

ZASULICH: By Christ you will though! You what? You
won't see a comrade who's travelled 4,000 miles to
ask for justice from the party ... what does it say?
(She scans the letter.) ... 'the party of the struggle
for the freedom, the dignity and the happiness of
man'? I'll fetch him in myself. You're a disgrace
to the party. A scourge and a monster.
*(ZASULICH storms towards the door. MARTOV calls her
name, hurries after her. Silence around the table.
Arguing on the stair outside. KRUPSKAYA picks up the
note, reads it. LENIN looks at TROTSKY.)*

LENIN: *(Very calm)* I have written to Plekhanov urging you
  be co-opted onto the *Iskra* board. *(Pause)* That is, if
  you still want it?

  (LENIN gestures at the door.)

TROTSKY: *(Calm too)* More than ever.

  *(KRUPSKAYA puts the letter down. She is simply moved.
  MARTOV in, without ZASULICH. He wipes his hands with
  a raspberry coloured handkerchief.)*

MARTOV: She ... won't come back. But she won't bring in
  Miliutin unless we send for him.

  (MARTOV sits down where ZASULICH sat.)

LENIN: Anything else?

MARTOV: *(Very tense)* Yes. I haven't finished. *(Pause)*
  I want to know what you intend to do about Bauman.

LENIN: Nothing.

MARTOV: *(Deliberately)* I think there should be an
  inquiry.

LENIN: Nadya, tell Comrade Martov Comrade Bauman's role
  in the *Iskra* network ...

MARTOV: *(Flashing)* I know his role ... don't play the
  Grandfather with *me*, comrade. It doesn't wear ...

LENIN: *(Hard)* Then don't be so *childish*. Bauman is an
  outstanding agent; not average; not good;
  outstanding. In party matters I would trust him above
  anyone I know. Now you're asking that he should be
  disciplined ... how? Expelled? ...

MARTOV: Yes, certainly, if it's true ...

LENIN: ... Expelled because of personal misdemeanours?
  Let me tell you, comrade, I rule an inquiry out of
  order, as being outside the competence of *Iskra* and
  detrimental to the interests of the party. If you
  want my *private* views on the matter you can have
  them ... privately.

MARTOV: *(Losing control)* You can't separate private from
     public like that, can't you see it man! We are what
     we *do* ... you, me, Bauman, all of us. Party morality
     is more than just loyalty to the party ... it's the
     highest level of ethical consciousness yet afforded
     the human species ...

LENIN: Metaphysics, Julius. Another time, perhaps, we
     may speculate. Just now we're trying to make the
     revolution *possible*.

     *(Silence. MARTOV disturbed, thrown, shivering a
     little, unused to being in conflict with LENIN.)*

MARTOV: So you'll do nothing.

LENIN: *(Standing)* I will do my duty. That's to say,
     I will protect Comrade Bauman from any move on your
     or anybody else's part to expel or discipline him.
     Be warned. *(To KRUPSKAYA)* I think we should go.

KRUPSKAYA: You go. I want to speak with Vera Ivanovna.

     *(LENIN stares at KRUPSKAYA, searching for betrayal.
     She touches his hand.)*

     I'll follow.

     *(LENIN nods. Leaves. MARTOV turns away from the
     table, his head in his hands. The front door bangs
     below. MARTOV is crying, shaking and trembling.
     KRUPSKAYA goes to him, presses his face into her
     belly, nurses him with shushing sounds. TROTSKY
     remains at the table, reaches for the suicide note
     with his pen, opens and reads it without taking it in
     his hands.)*

13.   INT.   LENIN BEDROOM.   NIGHT

*LENIN in bed, sick, at night. He's suffering from
inflammation of the nerve terminals of back and chest ...*

(shingles?) *naked, a thin sheet covering his loins and legs untidily, he bucks and rears, screams, his flesh red and blotched, his eyes fevered, remote.*

LENIN: *(Explaining crazily)* It's simple. See. I am the party. Right. Party organ ... unh? *(He indicates his head.)* ... unh? Central Committee ... *(He indicates a clenched fist.)* ... Right? Central Organ, Central Committee ... *(He begins again.)* See ... I am the party, eh? I am the party ... No, I ... mmm? mmm? ... Julius, you're not listening. *(Big shout.)* Martov!!!

(LENIN opens his eyes, blinks. KRUPSKAYA just in from kitchen, bowl of iodine and cloth in hands. She soothes him gently, begins to bathe his chest and back with the solution. LENIN, awake now, takes the pain with stiff face.)

KRUPSKAYA: You can't go on like this, Volodya. Let me get a doctor ... please.

LENIN: *(Quietly)* I want you to pack the trunks and prepare to leave.

KRUPSKAYA: We can't *leave*. You're ill, man ...

LENIN: *(Fierce)* Do it!

(Pause. Almost absentmindedly.)

Do it!

KRUPSKAYA: *(Dish of milk and bread)* Try to take some of this.

LENIN: *(Still in great pain)* Listen! Tell Martov I want to see him.

KRUPSKAYA: Julius is in Paris, en route for Geneva. There's a meeting of the Organising Committee.

LENIN: Did he call?

KRUPSKAYA: It blew up very suddenly. He left the day he heard of the meeting. *(Pause)* He's ... still hurt and bitter ...

LENIN: Who called the meeting of the Organising Committee?

KRUPSKAYA: I don't know. Rest, love.

LENIN: Rest? I'll rest when they rest! *(Pause)* It looks
as though Julius is making his bid for power.
*(LENIN says this with some sadness, resignation, as
well as foreboding.)*

KRUPSKAYA: No ... No, no.

LENIN: I say the party must be built like a fist, like a
brain balled. He wants a party like a saucerful of
calves' hearts put down for the cat. I must show
him he is wrong.
*(KRUPSKAYA covers LENIN gently with the thin sheet.
He closes his eyes. She stands, picks up the bowl.)*
(Eyes open) Thank you, comrade.
(KRUPSKAYA smiles, almost shy now, leaves.)

TELECINE 3:

Train coach and corridor. Day

*Train. LENIN and KRUPSKAYA in empty coach. Cutaways of
Swiss scenery. Every lurch of the train gives LENIN pain.
He is pale, drawn; sweat on forehead. KRUPSKAYA watches
him carefully. The train is slowing. A GUARD in the
corridor calls 'Secheron. Secheron, Geneva next stop.
Secheron, Secheron ...' BAUMAN, hard, heavy, pushes down
the corridor towards them. LENIN sees him, stands.*

LENIN: Bauman.

BAUMAN: There'll be police in Geneva. Are these yours?
*(LENIN nods. BAUMAN takes the cases easily, leads
the LENINS from the train.)*

14. INT. PLEKHANOV'S STUDY. GENEVA

Large, expensive, tastefully and expensively got out.
Double doors join it to the next room.
A view of mountains from the window. · The room is full of
books and 'objects'.

LENIN sits on a wooden chair. He is totally withdrawn:
almost rapt in his self-absorption. The double doors
open and PLEKHANOV appears. He is 45, the father of
Russian Marxism; aristocratic, elitist, intellectual,
vain; beautifully dressed, and with his own dignity. He
holds his hand out to greet LENIN. LENIN stands, takes
the hand.

PLEKHANOV: Ilyich! We meet again. Sit down, sit down.
     How are you? We were worried about you.

LENIN: *(Sitting)* Recovered ... thank you.
     (They study each other for several moments. They
     hide their distrust and dislike well.)

PLEKHANOV: Well, we're almost there. *(Pause)* You've
     worked hard.

LENIN: The operative word is 'almost', Georges.

PLEKHANOV: *(Ignoring him)* I've dreamed of this Congress
     for a quarter of a century. Do you know that? The
     Congress that will unify the party.

LENIN: ... With *Iskra* as its organisational and
     theoretical centre.

PLEKHANOV: Precisely, comrade.

LENIN: *(Softly)* But will it?

PLEKHANOV: What do you mean?

LENIN: We have forty-one votes out of a total of fifty-
     one, our principal opponents being the Jewish Bund,
     with five votes, and the Workers' Cause and the
     Southern Workers' factions with a further two votes
     each. Theoretically, we cannot fail to dominate the

Congress, push through our own resolutions and elect
our own people to the central committees of the
party. *(Pause)* The question remaining is: Who will
control *Iskra*?

(PLEKHANOV getting the measure of it now.)

PLEKHANOV: Doesn't *Iskra* speak with one voice?

LENIN: What do *you* think?

PLEKHANOV: You surprise me. I know of course there have
been personal frictions ... the Bauman affair, things
like that ... but surely there's no evidence of
ideological division, is there?

(LENIN pushes slightly, disliking the constraints.)

LENIN: Georges, Martov has tabled his own draft rules
for party membership ...

PLEKHANOV: *(Testily)* Yes, I have seen the agenda. *(Pause)*
I must say, I've read them both side by side, yours
and his, and I'm damned if I can see much difference
between them, if you allow for necessary differences
arising from stylistic capabilities.

LENIN: *(Resolute)* I'll tell you the difference in a
sentence, Georges. His rules allow anyone, any
opportunist, any windbag, any 'professor', any 'high
school student' to proclaim himself a party member,
while my rules - *our* rules, Georges - confine
membership to a narrow vanguard of professional
revolutionaries owing strict allegiance to the party
centre. That's the difference.

PLEKHANOV: *(Defensive now)* I'm not sure I'd accept the
interpretation of Martov's formulation that you
offer, Ilyich ...

LENIN: *(Deadly)* Well I think you should, Georges, because
comrade Martov certainly does.

(Silence)

PLEKHANOV: Are you sure?

LENIN: Perfectly.

PLEKHANOV: Then I'd better have a word with him.

LENIN: It might make matters worse. *(Pause)* I think we should simply see to it that his rules are defeated.

PLEKHANOV: How?

LENIN: Canvass. Argue. Persuade. Make sure of our votes. Secure them. Keep them hard if they look like softening. *(Pause)* I think we are the right people to lead the revolutionary party, Comrade Plekhanov. Theory and organisation drawn together like that ... *(He clasps his hands in front of him.)* What do you think?

(PLEKHANOV leans forward, places his hand on LENIN's.)

PLEKHANOV: Let's build the party, comrade.

(They look at each other for several moments, sealing the compact.)

I've always been fascinated by your hardness. It always seems so ... unrelative.

LENIN: *(Simply)* I was a gentle enough child.

PLEKHANOV: *(Trying the reassertion)* One thing I insist on. There will be no place for the man Trotsky on the new board of *Iskra*. He's too young and he's too arrogant.

LENIN: *(Finally, making the point)* All right, I withdraw the suggestion. *(He stands.)* Is it still London if the police stop us in Brussels?

PLEKHANOV: *(Standing)* That's right. *(He shows LENIN the door.)* I can't think why there should be trouble though *(PLEKHANOV's two teenage daughters, in riding habits, burst in.)*

Ah, you won't remember these two, will you?

(Takes them by shoulders. To girls:)

Say hello to comrade Lenin and go and get dressed,

you scamps.

(They laugh, say 'Bonjour, cher comrade' in turn, and leave the room.)

Well ... till Brussels ... Give my love to Nadya, won't you? Au revoir.

(LENIN leaves.

PLEKHANOV crosses to the upright piano, picks out a few bars from a Beethoven sonata with skill and precision.)

15. INT. BRUSSELS. LARGE OFFICE IN FLOUR WAREHOUSE. DAY

In which the Congress is convening.

A growing noise from the warehouse proper: shouting; laughter; occasional snatches of song.

The office is crowded. The Organising Committee and the Congress praesidium are trying to resolve matters of procedure before the first session. A good deal of all talking at once, as delegation leaders try to have their business recognised by chairman PLEKHANOV.

MARTOV, ZASULICH, POTRESOV, TROTSKY, ALEXANDROVA and several others sit round a large desk. LENIN, flanked by KRASIKOV, stands behind the seated PLEKHANOV. Before and all around them, the 'Economists' MARTINOV and AKIMOV, BROUCKERE of the Southern Worker, LIEBER and GOLDBLATT of the Jewish Bund, EGOROV, POPOV and others of the 'centre'.

LIEBER:*(Above the noise; angry)* So let me get this
straight, comrade. If the Jewish Bund refuses to surrender to party control over its *own* organisation, this Congress is prepared to expel us from the Party? Is that the meaning of Resolution 2 on the Agenda?

Now I'm asking you a straight question, comrade ...

PLEKHANOV: *(Lofty, in all the moil)* The answer is yes,

comrade. How many times must I *tell* you ... *yes*!!

LIEBER: Then I demand that this procedures committee rule
that the resolution be deferred. There should be a
commission. Some of my people have travelled the
length of Europe to be here ... We're party too,
you know.

MARTOV: *(Suddenly)* Shall we put that to a vote then?

LENIN: You know what our collective view is on the Bund,
comrade ...

MARTOV: *(Coolly)* We are now the Procedures Committee of
the Second Congress of the Russian Social Democratic
Party, comrade. Not the editorial board of the party
organ *Iskra*. *(To desk.)* Shall we vote it?
*(LENIN ready. PLEKHANOV uncertain. POTRESOV, next
to MARTOV, nods.)*

ZASULICH: Yes.

ALEXANDROVA: Yes.

PLEKHANOV: All right. Those in favour of deferring the
vote on the expulsion of the Bund.
(MARTOV, POTRESOV, AXELROD, ZASULICH, ALEXANDROVA.)
Against?
(LENIN, KRASIKOV, PLEKHANOV.)
Carried.

LIEBER: Thank God. Thank you, comrades.

PLEKHANOV: Next.
*(MARTINOV begins arguing for a similar concession for
his group.
LENIN and MARTOV glance at each other, impassive but
surly stares.
LENIN catches ZASULICH's eye.
POTRESOV's. His chill anger is patent.
BAUMAN in fast from the warehouse. He pushes through
the throng until he reaches LENIN, whispers. LENIN*

nods, bends over PLEKHANOV's shoulder, whispers.
PLEKHANOV nods, stands, bangs the desk with his feet.)
Comrades, comrades, listen to me.
(The din subsides. Sounds of movement, the odd shout
from next door.)
Six delegates have been arrested in their hotels. I'm
informed that the Belgian police are on their way to
break up the meeting. (Consternation, chatter.)
Comrades. The contingency plan is now effective.
Congress will convene in London in four days' time.
Go now.
(People move at speed.
PLEKHANOV begins gathering up Conference papers.)

LENIN: (To BAUMAN) Take care of Krupskaya. (BAUMAN
stands, frowning, emphatic.) Take care of Krupskaya.
(BAUMAN leaves, impassive, with KRUPSKAYA.
The room is almost empty. LENIN fills his briefcase
with papers from the table.
TROTSKY remains. LENIN looks up, sees him.)
Comrade. How fortunate, we'll travel together.
(Pause. TROTSKY says nothing.)
(Weighing words) I'm sorry I couldn't get Plekhanov
to co-opt you on to the board. There was nothing
I could do.

TROTSKY: No, of course.

LENIN: Nothing, comrade.

TROTSKY: No.

LENIN: (Ready) Well. Are you coming with me?

TROTSKY: No. (Pause) I'll make my own way.

LENIN: (Crossing to door, turning) Avoid ... personalities,
comrade. They could prove your downfall.
(He leaves. TROTSKY watches him.)

EVENING

The 22nd and crucial motion in progress.

The room is half tiered on two sides, with a
demonstration area and desk at the focus.

PLEKHANOV sits behind the demonstration desk, in the chair.
LENIN at a small table in front of the desk, as one of
the vice-chairmen.

As MARTOV speaks, we track around the room, clocking
faces, groupings, group titles crayoned on pieces of
cardboard ... All votes.

LENIN flicks from MARTOV to his 'support ...' The
sequence should suggest a hard-fought decision, when the
vote is taken ...

Some votes LENIN is unable to assign: TROTSKY, for
example; ALEXANDROVA and others of the original
Organising Committee.

MARTOV: If we adopt comrade Lenin's formula we shall be
throwing overboard a section of those who, even if
they cannot be directly admitted to an organisation,
are nevertheless Party members. We are a party of a
class, comrades. We must take care not to leave
outside the Party ranks people who consciously,
though perhaps not very actively, associate themselves
with our party. Indeed the more widespread the title
of Party member, the better.

(Applause from BUND, AKIMOV, MARTINOV, EGOVOV, POPOV,
ALEXANDROVA ... LENIN makes a note on a piece of
paper, missing nothing.)

For me, a conspiratorial organisation only has
meaning when it is enveloped by a broad
social-democratic working-class party.

LENIN: *(Shouting suddenly)* You're confusing a *party* with a *movement*, comrade. They're not the same thing.

MARTOV: *(Flaring as quickly)* No, comrade, it is you who
   are confused. You confuse the party with a bunch of
   professional ... thugs who will do your or somebody
   else's bidding without question ...

   *(Uproar. Applause for MARTOV: boos and shouts from
   hard Iskra-men (BAUMAN, KRASIKOV, LENGNIK, SHOTMAN,
   NOSKOV and others). LENIN white but perfectly
   controlled.)*

PLEKHANOV: *(Drily, as it dies)* Confine yourselves to
   argument, comrades. Reserve your abuse for the enemy.

MARTOV: I look forward to the day, comrades, when
   every striker, every demonstrator against the Tsar
   and his regime, accounts for his actions by stating:
   I am a member of the Social Democratic Party of
   Russia. If you share that hope, you will support my
   motion.

   *(MARTOV sits down, flushed, a little elated, dazed.
   Applause again, especially among the Bund.)*

PLEKHANOV: Comrade Lenin.

LENIN: *(Standing)* Thank you, Comrade Chairman. Comrades,
   you have heard the arguments ... Martov's and mine.
   What we're arguing about is both an image and a
   reality. If you accept my motion, you vote for
   coherence, organisation, discipline, above all, power
   at the *centre*. You will say, in effect, that it is
   essential to distinguish between those who belong to
   the Party and those who associate themselves with it.
   You make the necessary distinction between an *entire
   class*, shaped by *capitalism*, and its *vanguard*, the
   party. The title Party Member is a *fiction*, if it
   cannot be made to correspond to facts. Capitalism is
   bound to weigh down wide sections of the working class

with disunity, oppression and stultification. Social-Democracy seeks to lift the worker from his present level of consciousness to a genuinely *revolutionary* one. *But if we fail to recognise the distinction, there is no way we can achieve that end.* Vote for Martov's proposal, and you create a tea party, not a party of revolutionaries ready to lead a class into battle.

(LENIN sits down. Applause, counter-applause.)

PLEKHANOV: *(Reluctantly)* Well ... I suppose I should order that ... the vote be taken.

(He tries to catch LENIN's eye; fails.)

In favour of comrade Lenin's proposal on Party membershi

(Twenty-three votes. We need clock only key ones: LENIN's two, for example.)

Twenty ... three. And comrade Martov's ...?

(The Bund vote five; Economists and other rightists swell the number.

MARTOV's two hands go up.

A small knot of Iskra *people - ALEXANDROVA, for example - join in.*

ZASULICH, AXELROD, POTRESOV go up in turn.

And TROTSKY. KRUPSKAYA, who sits next to TROTSKY, can't look at him.)

(Grimly, writing it down) Twenty-eight. Comrade Martov's resolution carried.

(Hubbub. Shouting. Banging of fists on desks.)

The chair suggests a fifteen-minute adjournment.

(Carried by acclamation. LENIN sits silent, white, but held in.

MARTOV passes by his desk. Gives LENIN an odd smile.)

MARTOV: *(Tense, nervy)* Good fun!

LENIN: *(Bitterly)* Oh yes. There's nothing funnier than

watching a man commit political suicide.

MARTOV: *(Trying to laugh it off)* You think so?

LENIN: Today you have entered into an opportunistic
alliance with centre and right-wing elements. You
have surrendered your political credibility.

MARTOV: I doubt it. In any case, you left me little
option in the matter. You forced me to beat you.

LENIN: *(Bleakly)* You have won a battle, comrade. The
war has only just begun.

*(MARTOV limps out. Hall empty. LENIN surrounded by
Iskra hards: principally BAUMAN, KRASIKOV, LENGNIK,
SHOTMAN, NOSKOV.)*

Full caucus meeting tonight, to decide on our list
for the Central Committee and the Party Council.
7.30 sharp. Questions? *(None)* Bauman, when does the
commission on the Bund propose reporting back?

BAUMAN: Next week sometime, according to Tupuridze.

LENIN: I want the report and the vote tomorrow morning.
You see Tupuridze, I'll see Plekhanov. Do it now.

17. CAUCUS MEETING. EVENING

*A small, cramped room. LENIN in chair; a dozen 'hards',
including BAUMAN, KRASIKOV, SHOTMAN, LENGNIK, NOSKOV,
KRZHIZHANOVSKY, TUPURIDZE.*

*KRUPSKAYA as secretary. A broom-handle has been wedged
in the double swing door handles, to lock it.*

*One of the 'hards' stands guard by it. The door shifts
slightly as MARTOV, locked out, bangs and calls on the
other side. He has been there protesting since the
meeting started. His tone is now a little desperate,
unreal.*

MARTOV: *(Off)* Let me *in!* I demand to be admitted. It is
   directly forbidden by party rules to exclude members
   of the executive from caucus meetings.
   *(MARTOV goes on with this throughout the scene that
   follows.)*

LENIN: *(Dictating to Krupskaya)* ... Comrade Lengnik ...
   Comrade Noskov. *(Turning to meeting.)* That concludes
   the lists for the central committees. I don't need
   to remind you that the voting will be *solid*. We have
   outlived the wavering days. The Bund ... *(Pausing,
   looking for Tupuridze.)* I've seen Plekhanov. The
   Bund problem will be taken first thing tomorrow. Is
   your commission able to report, Tupuridze?

TUPURIDZE: It will be by morning.

LENIN: Good ... No problems?

TUPURIDZE: No problems.

LENIN: Good. *(Standing)* That's all. *(To man at door.)*
   Let comrade Martov in when the comrades have left,
   will you?
   *(They disperse swiftly, brushing past MARTOV in the
   doorway, the doorman's big hand on his chest.
   KRUPSKAYA tidies her files.)*

KRUPSKAYA: Do you want *me?*
   (LENIN shakes his head.
   *She leaves. She meets MARTOV a few paces into the
   room. He barely sees her. Stands staring at LENIN.
   LENIN is writing something on a piece of paper. Looks
   up at length.)*

MARTOV: *(Pleading)* What is *happening*, Volodya?

LENIN: I don't know what you mean. I was in caucus ...

MARTOV: *(Almost screaming)* You had me locked out. *(He
   tries to get himself together.)* Why?

LENIN: Simply ... you no longer belonged to the caucus.

100

MARTOV: Why? Because my motion won the majority in
        congress?
LENIN: No. Because your 'majority' was based upon an
        openly opportunistic alliance with the 'swamp', with
        the right and centre elements of the party, the
        elements we as a tendency have been fighting for the
        last year.
MARTOV: There was no ... *alliance*. I haven't spoken to
        the Bund since Brussels. Believe it!
        (Silence.

        LENIN impassive.

        MARTOV gets closer, gathering.)

        Volodya ... comrade, there are no fundamental
        differences between us. *(Pause)* Can't we simply sit
        down and talk it out? We share the *same* vision,
        comrade ... We spent the whole night talking, the
        night before Siberia ... do you remember? On and on.
        Building the vision ... *(Pause)* Tell me what I should
        do.
LENIN: *(Softly)* I can't do that, comrade. You must find
        that for yourself. The *choices* are clear. If you are
        not to be tainted with the Bund for the rest of your
        days, you must make it clear tomorrow that your
        position is as it always was, that total authority
        over the activities of members shall be exercised
        by the party centre. (Catching MARTOV's surprise.)
        The Procedures Committee have decided that the
        question of the Bund should be tackled at once.
MARTOV: But the Bund commission hasn't reported ...
LENIN: That's being taken care of. *(Pause)* If, on the
        other hand, you decide that you need the votes of the
        Bund and other centre elements to gain control of the
        party, you will be exposed as an opportunist and a

counterfeit revolutionary. *(Pause)* The choice is yours.

MARTOV: *(With growing hauteur)* There can be no question of my cynically changing my position on national autonomy within the party. My position is identical with yours, as you very well know, comrade.

LENIN: The point is not that *I* know it. The point is that everyone in the party, *including* the Bund, knows it.

(Pause again.

MARTOV is wondering whether the rupture has begun mending.)

MARTOV: I wanted to ... talk to you ... about the composition of the central committees ... There is good argument for building on the existing Organising Committee ...

LENIN: There is nothing to talk about. We have decided our lists.

(MARTOV stunned a little, breathless.

He turns away, walks a few paces to the door. A delayed reaction.)

MARTOV: I see. I see. *(Pause. Vicious now.)* Have you made recommendations on who should be elected Dictator of the Party too? Eh? Or will you be able to manage without that?

(LENIN folds his papers away, walks past MARTOV without a glance, leaves the room.)

(As LENIN passes) I asked you a question, comrade. Vera Zasulich was right; Potresov was right, Axelrod was right. You think you're Robespierre ... that's what they think ... By God they're right.

(The door swings shut.

MARTOV kicks a chair over, in a swift freak of anger. The following morning. Congress in progress. The

groupings - MARTOV's, LENIN's - now very clearly
delineated in the way they sit.)

TUPURIDZE: *(Winding up)* ... I repeat, the commission this
Congress set up to inquire into the question whether
the Jewish Workers' Alliance could lawfully remain
within the party without subjecting itself to party
disciplines is of the opinion: (a) that no grounds
can be found why the Bund should not accept party
constraints and (b) that therefore Congress should
proceed to vote at once on whether the Bund should be
allowed to exercise rights in the party and, in
particular, in this Congress. *(He sits down.)*

PLEKHANOV: Thank you, comrade. Questions?

(LIEBER, leader of the Bund, on his feet.)

LIEBER: I must protest, Comrade Chairman. We were given
unequivocal assurances by the Procedures Committee in
Brussels ...

BAUMAN: Out of order, Comrade Chairman!

KRASIKOV: 'This man has no right to speak, Comrade
Chairman,' eh?

(Hubbub, as hard Iskra men keep up a flow of
interruptions.

LENIN stands up; his men subside.)

LENIN: Comrade Bauman is right, Comrade Chairman. The
commission's recommendation is that we proceed
directly to the vote.

MARTOV: *(Nervous, uncertain)* The commission cannot
determine what Congress may or may not do, Comrade
Chairman.

PLEKHANOV: Very well. Would Congress like to hear
argument on this matter or move at once to the vote?
Show, please. Those in favour of moving to the vote?
(The Iskra vote, about twenty, solid.)

PLEKHANOV: *(Repeating himself, very deliberately)* Those
in favour of moving forward to a vote ...
(AXELROD puts hand up; ZASULICH, TROTSKY, POTRESOV ...
MARTOV joins them ... the 'centre' follow suit.
About forty hands lifted now.)
Carried.

LIEBER: I protest, Chairman! This is monstrous.
(Counter-boos and hisses.)

PLEKHANOV: *(Over din)* And now the vote itself. Those
against the Bund's being allowed to remain within
the Party, please show ...
(The same procedure.
MARTOV trapped, unable to run risk of being labelled
a political opportunist, but conscious that he is
voting his own majority away.)
Forty ... one. An overwhelming majority for
expulsion.
(The Bund consults.
LIEBER stands up.
Some jeering from the 'hards'. LENIN impassive.)

LIEBER: There is no question of staying, comrades. The
insult and humiliation you have dealt us will live
with us many a day. Like you, we dream of and work
for the socialist revolution. All we have asked is
that we be allowed to do it in our own language with
our own people. You deny us that basic right,
because of some ... Napoleon who craves after personal
power. *(A storm of booing and hissing.)* It's true!
See it now before it's too late. *(PLEKHANOV calls for*
order; gets it finally.) Well ... we will continue to
fight for the revolution ... with or without the aid
of the party we helped to form.
(LIEBER leaves.

The others file out with him, in silence.)

MARTINOV: The Workers' Cause group wish to demonstrate
solidarity with the Bund against the ... dictatorial
tendencies that are emerging inside the party
apparatus. We hereby withdraw from the Congress.
*(MARTINOV and AKIMOV withdraw. Cheering from the
'hards'. MARTOV approaches LENIN's table.)*

MARTOV: You see. If history seeks an opportunist, it
will not be in my direction that it will look,
comrade.

LENIN: *(Smiling icily)* If it does not label you an
opportunist, it may well conclude that you're a fool.
(Pause) I believe it may very well call you both.
*(Sequence of minimally notated mixes, in which
Congress votes in LENIN's lists for Central Committee
and Party Council. Each time, MARTOV's group abstain.
PLEKHANOV duly announces the election of the Iskra
'hards' ... LENGNIK, KRZHIZHANOVSKI, NOSLOV - Central
Committee, etc.)*

PLEKHANOV: Elections for the board of *Iskra*, the party
journal. Comrade Lenin?
*(LENIN stands at his desk. He waits for the Congress,
seething and boiling, to subside.)*

LENIN: You have already, in an earlier vote, affirmed the
place of *Iskra* as the ideological centre of our party.
It is now our task to elect its editorial board, whose
role it will be to create political guidelines for
party action in the struggle against the Russian state.
(Pause) I have, as you know, been associated with
Iskra since its birth three years ago. And I think I
can say, with all modesty, that the work we have done
on the *Iskra* front has been of decisive influence in
the shaping and development of our party. But it is

the future, not the past, that calls us on. Times change: capacities change; objective circumstances change. What our party journal requires now is a small nucleus of trained ideologues and organisers capable of launching the work far and wide across the Russian empire. *(Pause. Very resolute.)* It is for this reason that I propose that we should decrease the number of seats from six to three; and further, I nominate, as *Iskra* editors, myself, Comrade Plekhanov ... and ... Comrade Martov.

(He sits down. Stunned silence, at least in MARTOV ranks. MARTOV gets up, rather dazed, unable to take it in.)

MARTOV: *(Weakly)* This is not possible, Comrade Chairman. Have we not already voted for the continuance of the *Iskra* ...

(VERA ZASULICH begins to scream; like a Cossack charging.)

ZASULICH: You ... bastard! You dirty stinking bastard! Jesus God, if I had a pistol I'd blow your rotten brains out! You're not a comrade, you're a dictator ... You're a bloody *Tsar*. I see your game, Lenin. By hook or by crook, isn't it. Anyway so long as it's your way, with your 'hard' men all around you. What do you care about loyalty ... and service ... and dedication ...? I've spent a lifetime ... so has Axelrod, Potresov ... of devotion to this party. And now you ... cut us off. Just like that. To fall into the swamp. *(Broken already.)* You are no man to lead this great movement ... *(To PLEKHANOV)* And you ... you whom I have worshipped as a great mind and comrade ... one day this man will eat you for breakfast ...

(ZASULICH walks out, avoiding KRUPSKAYA's outstretched

hand of sympathy. The 'hards' hurl epithets and
derisory shouts after her.)

MARTOV: *(With dignity)* May I remind those comrades who
now revile comrade Zasulich ... that you are reviling
the comrade who shot the infamous Colonel Trepov of
the Moscow secret police, when he ordered the
flogging of workers who had demonstrated against the
Tsar.

*(Derision tails off. The conference waits for
MARTOV's move.)*

(Quietly) I refuse to accept nomination under these
arrangements.

PLEKHANOV: You are not allowed to refuse, comrade, under
the rules you yourself voted in only days ago.

MARTOV: *(Very quiet)* I will not serve with *that man*!
That man is ... not a good man!

*(MARTOV walks out. POTRESOV and AXELROD follow.
TROTSKY stands.)*

TROTSKY: *(Measured, eloquent)* If this is comrade Lenin's
'image of the party', then I want no part of it. What
he has done today shames and degrades all of us.
Zasulich and Axelrod in particular have fought all
their lives to build the party. And now here, on the
brink of success, they are ruthlessly cut off and
sent out into the wilderness, to satisfy the
insatiable lust for power of one individual. *(Waves of
protest, etc. TROTSKY listens to it.)* Comrades, we
are privileged to be listening to the sound of party
debate - new style.

*(TROTSKY leaves with a flourish, to jeers. The
remainder of MARTOV's group follow him.)*

LENIN: *(Calmly)* I so move, Comrade Chairman.

Ext. Marx's grave (Note: as it was Nov. 1903) in
Highgate

*Around the grave, split into factions, LENIN's to the
left, MARTOV's to the right; PLEKHANOV in the centre.
They stand in silence. We scan the strain and tension in
hands and faces. Finally ...*

PLEKHANOV: *(Almost under breath)* We dedicate this great
... unifying Congress ... to the memory of the great
man whose body is laid herein.

*(They stand on a little longer. LENIN flanked by
'hards', BAUMAN and KRASIKOV prominent. KRUPSKAYA
stands at the back, staring at ZASULICH who is
distraught and totally destroyed.)*

(Furling his umbrella) Well, comrades. Good luck,
wherever your work may take you ...

*(PLEKHANOV steps back onto the path. ZASULICH,
AXELROD, POTRESOV join him in a group; some small
departing chat. The 'hards' drift away. Some
handshakes from LENIN etc.)*

KRUPSKAYA: I must speak with Vera Ivanovna.

LENIN: Leave it ...

KRUPSKAYA: *(Levelly)* I must.

*(LENIN nods finally. KRUPSKAYA hurries off after
ZASULICH. TROTSKY approaches LENIN.)*

TROTSKY: I did what I had to.

LENIN: But what you had to do was not what had to be done.

TROTSKY: At least, I did not destroy the party.

LENIN: *(Slowly)* Yesterday the party was *made*, not
destroyed. What is more, history will prove it to be
the only party - the only sort of party - capable of
capturing state power. You seem to think a party is
an organisation for the deliberation of complex moral

choices, a sort of political sewing circle. *(Pause)*
You will not find the Tsar and von Plehve, and Trepov
and Witte, and the state apparatus, sitting around
'deliberating moral choices' ... They are *organising*
their defence ... There is only one slogan that will
defeat them. *Salus populi lex suprema est.* In
revolutionary language, the success of the revolution
is the supreme law. Until you can say that, comrade,
and mean it, history will have no use for you.
*(TROTSKY looks over his shoulder. Only MARTOV remains
at the graveside.)*

TROTSKY: I suppose it will depend who writes the history.
*(TROTSKY walks off. LENIN and MARTOV left. They are
about twenty feet apart. They look at each other for
several moments, openly, without venom. MARTOV wants
to speak but controls it. He turns eventually, limps
off. LENIN watches him.*
*LENIN stands by the tomb, alone, in L.S. C.U., he
stares at the head of Marx. Crows flap past,
unexpected.*
*NICHOLAS, on his estates at Tsarskoe Selo, aims, fires.
The huge flock of crows flaps on across the sky.
C.U. frowning. We hear him reload.*
KRUPSKAYA rejoins LENIN.)

KRUPSKAYA: Zasulich wept. She can't understand why you've
done what you have done.
*(LENIN looks at her, pushes stray floats of hair out
of her eyes.)*

LENIN: Remember Minusinsk. Remember the peasant crouched
over in the field? It was impossible to say what he
was doing. And when we'd walked across the field and
reached him, we saw at once that he was sharpening
his scythe on a stone. From the path it was

impossible to say ...

KRUPSKAYA: She has nothing left, she said.

LENIN: *(Quietly)* There is nothing to be done about that.
    *(They look at each other. Turn, walk off towards
    the gate, two simple bourgeois on a Sunday morning
    stroll.*
    Fade out.)